ISLAM

Facts and Fiction

And The Fight For

EGYPT

By

Mohamed F. El-Hewie

In the memory
of

Asma Beltagy.

Murdered by

General Abdul Fattah El-Sissi's snipers

On August 14, 2013

In
The massacre of Rabaa Al-Adawiya Square
Cairo, Egypt

TABLE OF CONTENTS

Introduction

This is the third book written by the author on the Egyptian Revolution. The other two books are: (1) "Chain Reaction: Egypt's Revolt 2011 Illustrated" and (2) "A Matter of FAITH: The Islamic Spring".

The three books comprise the views of an Egyptian immigrant to the United Stated, left Egypt in 1984 while Mubarak was in power, never returned home due to Mubarak's pervasive corruption and destruction of Egypt. About ten million Egyptians face the same fate of the author of alienating the Nile Valley and never return. Many more millions of Egyptians could not flee from the grip of oppression and corruption of Mubarak, some drowned while attempting to arrive to the European shores. The only exceptions were Mubarak's two sons who were helped by their father to work abroad while their father squeezed the life out of 82 million remaining Egyptians.

To be fair, Egypt has taken the path of decay and destruction soon after the 1967's war with Israel and as a result of Nasser's hard-headed politics of spreading revolution, nationalism, and socialism in the Middle East. Thus, Hosni Mubarak was stuck with the heavy burden of fixing failing state about which he lacked any experience in handling.

Mubarak's iron-grip on Egypt was not loosened by revolutionary resistance as it was by his aging, detachment from reality, and his wife's delusion in inheriting Egypt to her son Gamal Mubarak. Gamal would have succeeded his father without much resistance had not saboteurs managed to instigate killings of civilians, which ignited tsunamis of anger and violence.

The author described both the defunct regime of Mubarak and the newly elected Islamist regime from the point of view of a layman affected by his country politics from afar.

In this book, the author adopts the same approach of pacing together the pieces of the puzzle of the military coup of the reverse revolution against Morsi, the newly elected president, and the return of Mubarak's old regime to power.

The entire book depends entirely on news fed to the author's family connection in Egypt, open Internet sources, and daily news and interviews. It is written in the heat of the moment and carried all emotions towards a wounded nation and people by one of them living thousands of miles away.

Mohamed F. El-Hewie
New Jersey, USA
November 1, 2013

CHAPTER 1

Facts Favoring Islam

Essence of Islam

The power of Islam rises from its programming of the human mind by the logic, reasoning, and eloquence of Quranic doctrine, which places Allah as a supreme legislator who inspired his messengers, ending by Prophet Muhammad, to outline those heavenly laws to mankind.

In such concise definition of the mission of Islam, islamists confront great animosity on many fronts:

On one front, all those **raised to reject Muhammad** regardless of the merits of his mission comprise of a majority of non-Islamic nations which teach that their own savior and God were the only way to salvation. Those remote enemies of Islam might inflict their hatred by treating muslim immigrants unfavorably or through crusading invasions such as the cases of supporting Israel at the expense of the Palestinians, the invasion of Iraq and Afghanistan. There is almost no tenable solution to getting anti-Muhammad to change hearts and there might not even be a reason or benefit to gain from doing so, since geographic barriers suffice to dilute the danger of remote hostilities.

On a second front, islamists confront greater enemies among those educated and nurtured to reject Gods that cannot demonstrate material trails that could fulfill their immediate gratification. The hurdle of defining the concept of God to those trained and coached to think that the **scientific method** was too potent to sanction the concepts of soul, mind, divine, morality, creation, purpose of life, or fatalism, might be one of persistent persuasion. Most adherent or advocates of the scientific method in the realm of defining God lack the understanding of the scope of the scientific method.

Border-line muslims are educated to believe that Muhammad's views were restricted to his day and place. Those are discouraged by the heavy demands of close-minded radical islamists calling for strict adherence to the five rituals of Islam without addressing the pressing injustice and unfairness inflicted on the masses by improperly elected government.

In this grim views of oppressed and impoverished millions of muslims and detached and demanding few perfectionist islamists, it was inevitable to resort to violence as the only available option in changing the long lasting oppressive governing system. Those are required to adhere to the basic five rituals of Islam found Jihad, riots, and protesting the most effective ritual and mean to bring social justice, before heavenly imposed Islamic rituals could do them any good.

On the third front, islamists confront the vast and prevalent ignorance of their own top leaders. Those confuse the literal statements of Quran with their figurative meanings. Among those was **Mahamoud Shaaban**, a professor of Arabic Rhetoric in Al-Azhar University. Shaaban held a copy of the Quran, walked among a crowd and announced on live-TV that he had in his hand a proof from the Quran and the early interpreters of Quran that those of the **Egyptian Front for**

Rescue (which was an opposition organization to Mohammed Morsi, headed by Mohammed ElBaradie, Hamdeen Sabbahie, and Amr Mousa) should be killed for turning Egypt into chaos and failure.

Shaaban was arrested and his trial was set to deal with his intent to spread retribution against opponents of Islamic Project. Not too long after Shaaban has engaged in his extreme reaction that Morsi was removed by military coup and islamists were thrown in prisons by fabricated charges, their TV stations were closed, and their properties confiscated.

Sheikh Mahamoud Shaaban's statement and his logic was perfectly sound and inevitably the only way to spare Egypt anarchy. But, his sudden announcement and its naked truth turned the wolves against him. Only Salafis supported their courageous man. Had those few instigators named by Mahamoud Shaaban were removed or punished, thousands of lives would have been spared and Egypt would have avoided the military coup. But Mahamoud Shaaban was the prophet rejected by his own people, in the same fashion Moses failed to board his enemies on his boat.

All those moderate Islamists who rejected Mahamoud Shaaban's radical Fatwa, will carry him physically on their shoulders in Rabaa Al-Adawiya Square, as he showed up to remind them with their failure to heed his advice. Mahmoud Shaaban's comical style and his restless body movements annoy his audience and might have undermined his ability to convey a solemn fact that **anarchy will burn us all**.

1.1. Figurative Verses of Quran

Despite many poor examples of islamists and many unwise decisions made under the name of Islam (such as the terrible crimes committed by Al-Qaeda's organization that left many innocent people dead), the richness of Quranic **figurative laws of logic and reason** empowered billions of followers of Islam to isolate the extreme violations of the spirit of Islam from mainstream eloquent logic of honoring mankind by the consistent wisdom of Quran.

1.1.1. Creator and Creatures

What are those consistent laws of Quranic heavenly wisdom?

That man and his creator are bound by a contract that man strives to do good and right in return for gaining rewards of peaceful soul and mind, in life and heavens. The heavenly contract is deemed inviolable.

It is the censor of conscience attributed to heaven's creator.

Those violate such bond with the creator are punished in life and hell. Punishments depend on deliberate and willful intention to commit wrong versus and existing mitigating circumstances. Those might compel a reasonable person to deviate from right and good deeds.

How such contract between the creator and created be enforced?

The **concept of the creator** was settled before any credible civilization succeeded in uniting groups of people into structured communities. All claims that God has no address to be found, no trace to ascribed to, face the imminent fact that humans cannot rise from void, cannot live without purpose.

Our intellect cannot be subjected to any crude or highly structured scientific methods. As such a scientific method devised to verify empirical evidence is per se a power given from God to man. It allows him to sort out reality from fiction. Man cannot create his own intellect and power to resolve conflict from void.

What constitutes hell or heaven?

The mechanism by which a **creator engages in the fate of the created** is not hard to discern from the highly complicated design and function of human minds. One cannot assume that a villain could get away with his wrong deeds and enjoy the fruits of wrongs throughout the course of his life. Mostly, a villain would fall in his own wrong plot by virtue of his own twisted logic.

Let us consider a benignly accepted lifestyle of earning easy living with comfortable accommodation, versus earning living through the tedious labor of farming and hard labor. One cannot deny that hard labor and struggle empowers the laborer with greater experience and understanding of reality over the earner detached from engaging activities.

The logic and reason of Quran figuratively includes such vast relations between **deeds and gains** regardless of the social stigma associated with immediate gratification. Would a thief engaged in robbery lead a healthy life style with his improperly grabbed booty versus a hard working honest earner living within his own limits?

How far can one go to implicate the creator in the fate of the created?

Linear logic implies that the creator should have another creator, leading to cyclical argument over the origin of life.

The most we could claim is that man's fate is determined mostly by man's intellect and that a trustworthy religion should appeal to such high intellect.

In that realm, Islam comprises the **greatest pool of intellectual exercises** that challenge the human mind. In all those Quranic challenges, Allah is proposed as a supreme legislator. Allah has the ability to punish and reward, the ability to draw the bounds of straight path for good deeds and the twisted path for wrong deeds, explain the reasons and merits of each path.

Muslims are thus left with a vast **array of figurative laws,** which inspire the minds of billions of followers of Islam to argue and reach their own conclusions regarding many issues that confront mankind.

Those inspirations amount to the global consensus of muslims derived directly from the Quranic eloquent stating of figurative rules of conduct and retribution. Those are allegedly passed from God to mankind through the inspiration of Prophet Muhammad.

1.1.2. Quranic Canons of Deeds and Intent

The merits of those Quranic laws reside in offering young muslim kids with 6236 versus, falling into 114 suras of the Quran.

Many able muslim families invest in teaching their children those 6236 verses between the ages of 6 and 11 such that the child expands his /her word library to 77797 words over 5 years of childhood. That results in life-long experience where the child has long ingrained **repertoire of ideas, words, and experiences.** Those interact with newly encountered challenges in adolescence and adulthood that determine the final course the person follows in life.

The debate over the merits of those figurative Quranic laws, or whether a child nurtured on the grounds that Allah sets universal laws of conduct, would indoctrinate the child to believe in **superstition and myth** rather than relying on empirical methods that achieve verifiable and reproducible outcome, is one of conjecture not facts. For, there is no value in religious teaching if it lacks consistency and concord with reality.

A child nurtured on suggestions that God created us and God set the laws by which we live would still question the **mechanism and means** of involving God in workable life situations.

In contrast, a child left to the odds of **secular upbringing**, spoiled with toys, unlimited Internet and TV access, and education through government educational institutions, must search for parallel or different riches equivalent to those of Quran. That child would lack the contact exposure to adults, who could inspire the child to care about the most intriguing concept of **creation, God, and the purpose of life.**

One cannot fairly prove that a child nurtured by an ardent believer in God or in the chaos and chance of the theory of evolution would adopt those ideas and beliefs unconditionally or assertively. In all faiths, people do not cease questioning the means, facts, and reliability of believing in the **divine.**

The belief in the divine explains the fact that the scientific method is entirely excluded from **fundamental issues in life** such as choice of parents, race, gender, time at birth, choice of country of origin, color of skin, or course and end of education, or the determination of the longevity of the individual. All humans lack any **deterministic authority** on many of those stated issues and must submit to the role of the divine embodied in the collective intellect of the community.

In a secular setting, a woman could bear a child outside the wedlock with social and state endorsement. That would lead to different interpersonal bonding than in settings where marriage and family are viewed as divine requirement for bringing a child to life. Such collective community intellect cannot be ignored in regard of the prevalence of very **particular views** over family structure in Christian, Islamic, and other non-Semitic religions.

1.1.3. Heaven and Hell

The doctrine of rewards and punishments is wired in the genetic codes of living creatures; in the same manner it governs inert matter. Those are formulated by Isaac Newton in the seventeenth century that actions are opposed by equal reactions.

It is that repertoire of figurative laws of Islam that forms a **background** upon which seeds of many and unexpected talents could be planted, asserted, and nurtured to maturity. The background of Islamic upbringing entails plenty of **prohibitions and encouragements** all of which pool into the concept of promoting good will and good nature and discouraging destructive and risky behavior.

This **prohibitive-facilitative Islamic doctrine** transcends the teachings memories of thousands of years of cumulative human experience into the future generation, which is wired genetically to discern the common trends shared by mankind across most cultures.

At this cross roads of outgrowing previously **ingrained Islamic indoctrination** and entering the stage of inquisitive adult maturity, some learners are fixated on the literal meaning on the heavenly laws. Others weigh in the figurative inclusion of vast scope of wisdom rather than getting entangled into the materialistic events of depicted scenarios.

Involving a child in issues of creation, creator, and purpose of life shapes the future of **child development** and **mental growth.**

As the child evolves through the stages of **concrete thinking**, onto **role identification**, ending with adult maturity, the child faces the challenges of mental, physical, emotional, and intellectual maturity. Each challenge requires age-limit involvements, access, and training, so as to probe the ability and potentials of the growing person.

Unfortunately, the vast majority of children in the world are held to the very limited **resources and convictions** of their parents and the immediate resources of their neighboring community. To that extent, a child born in wealthy white American suburbs might have access to academic and nurturing resources; where as those in Latino and Black neighborhood are deprived of.

Yet, in both cases, mostly state and town politics determine the course of action that shapes the path of growth and development of the learner. In both cases, the learner is mostly a product of **assembly-line educational systems**. The criteria of assessing the better way of upbringing and educating young learners are also products of **assembly-line** process in which the community determines how to prepare the growing youth to meet its own needs and demands. While such pragmatic planning serves the immediate goals of the community, it deals with the most precious human resources as a commodity rather than a pool of unprecedented talents that could change the future of the nation.

In such **predetermined setting** of preparing the new learners, few uplifting factors could breed exceptional individuals. Those could be **exceptionally supporting parents**, or accidental exposure to new activities and cultures

In my personal experience, **divine intervention** brought me in an era and place in Egypt, led by the ambitious leader, Gamal Abdul Nasser. He implemented the socialist program of enlisting young children into athletic trainings. Those gathered the most talented figures of the nation in close contacts with youth. That narrow and accidental window of time, in 1966-1967, altered the course of my life far and beyond any other factor in education, family, or otherwise. The newly acquired exposure in 1966 resulted into my first published book in 2003 on the special topic of

11

weightlifting. Then, I already achieved postdoctoral education in engineering and doctoral training and licensure in medicine and surgery.

1.2. The Vocalization of Quranic Verses

The brilliant structural vocalization of Quranic verses distinguished the figurative treasures of Quran above the Biblical verses by creating billions of **readers** and **reciters** throughout the history of Islam.

The new art of reciting Quran born with the birth of Islam created a fascinating **world of voices and meanings** that extended over fourteen hundred years. To date, recitation and vocalization of Quran imposes new dimensions of faith and religion.

Listeners and learners can connect to the style and feeling of the reciter. This emphasizes the intended meaning of Quranic verses.

Quranic vocalists cannot engage in non-Quranic materials and are rebuked if they deviated from serving the content subject of Quran in order to emphasize their personal singing abilities.

Standardized vocalization of the Quranic verses created a homogeneous and global phenomena of **unified tongue** and articulation across geographic landscape, from Indonesia, in the south east Asia, to Spain, in the south west Europe.

In almost every village in Egypt and for many generations, many Quranic reciters compete in the mastery of the contents and vocals of Quran. Such vocalization practices strengthened the **community memory** of the Quranic sceneries. In every village's mosque one could easily spot a reciter able and willing to catch any deviation from the Quranic verses, committed inadvertently by the imam or lecturer in Quran.

Many of those reciters of Quran resort to **singing, composition,** and **poetry,** helped by the encyclopedic contents of Quranic verses. Among those is sheikh **Imam Issa.** (Imam is his name not his title).

Imam Issa was expelled from the profession of recitation of Quran after being caught sitting in a café shop listening to the radio's recitation of Quran, in 1945. Then, radio's recitation of Quran was considered improper tampering with the revered and restrained vocalization of Quran. Imam Issa was blind, living in Cairo, the most crowded city in Egypt. For a blind person, café shops scattered on every street corner in Cairo were rest-stops, where he could sit, wait for guide or companion to lead him home. His employer, the Assembly of Quran reciters, knew that very well. But, Imam Issa's mentor has passed away, his enemies and rivals harbored great resentment for the two. Thus, Imam was fired by fabricated charges that he was unworthy to recite Quran by virtue of his liberal sanction of the radio broadcasting, and by sitting in public places with common people to do the unthinkable degradation of the stature of a sheikh. Imam Issa became towering figure in **music composition and singing**.

The ordeal of sheikh Imam unfolded into two main ordeals. Imam created a new school of radio for composition of **songs and poetry** that combines the Quranic canons with humors, sarcasm, dancing, and political critics. The mix of Quranic figurative ideas with Egyptian vernacular captivated millions of listeners across the Middle East.

Coating Quranic canons in humor attracted new crowds of listeners and paved the way to widespread public unrest of people seeking **liberation from tyrants**. Sheikh Imam Issa was labeled as national security agitator and threat on community peace. Sheikh Imam Issa was arrested many times and thrown in prisons for eighteen years.

In such terrible injustice inflicted on a blind man by his own fellow reciters and later by the government that viewed Imam Issa as outspoken agitator, the blind sheikh was struck by diabetes mellitus. The chronic debilitating medical illness requires great care for life. Imam died from the complications of diabetes.

Another exceptional example was the famous singer Um Kalthoum, who earned the title of the "Eastern Star". **Um Kalthoum** developed a powerful vocalization of Quranic words. Those enabled her captivate millions of listeners for half a century of conservative and rich singing.

Among the famous stories in contemporary Egyptian history of music was between the composer **Fareed Al-Atrash** and Um Kalthoum. Freed complained that Um Kalthoum was the only respected, revered, highly educated singer in the history of Arabic heritage, that all new women singers were either shallow, immature, lacking public respect or appeal despite their singing talent. Um Kalthoum reneged on all promises she made to sing to Fareed Al-Atrash, despite assuring him that she was motivated to sing his materials.

The combined effect of intellectual repertoire of ideas in the Quranic verses and the structured vocalization of the contents of such repertoire distinguished Islam from Christianity and Judaism. The **personal performance** of the reciter obviates the need for musical equipments. It restricts Islamic lecturing to the content of recitation to Quranic verses.

The tendency of many Islamic lecturers to entangle **individual poetry or composition** with Quranic verses always raises disdain and rejection among the audience. As Quran is attached to Allah and his prophet Muhammad, any poetic intermingling with Quranic verses are construed as tampering with the heavenly contents of Quran.

Among those notorious violators of the above rule of intermingling of Quran with poems are the two sheikhs **Ben Laden** and **Ayman Al-Zawahiri**. Both men entertained long poems in support for their subjective interpretation of Quran. The recorded broadcastings of the two men prevented live-interaction of audience, which would alert the lecturer to refrain from individual poems, adhere to the spirit of Quran.

Farther, intermingling rhyming poems with Quranic vocalization defeats the conserved standards of delivery of Quranic contents according to their intended context. It shifts the attention to the emotional bias of the poet and the advocate of such poetry rather than adhering to Quranic concepts. As we stated above, sheikh Imam Issa was fired from his job, as a reciter of Quran, for listening to radio broadcasting of Quran recited by reciters like Ben Laden and Zawahiri.

The simplicity of reliance of personal skills alone helped spread Islam in many remote geographical localities where residential technical infra structures are modest.

Today, with all modern technological advances, the two most **powerful assets for any politician**, speaker, or leader required to captivate the hearts and souls of muslims are:

(1) Repertoire of ideas and words.
(2) Ability to vocalize and articulate Quranic ideas.

No civilized democratic society has been led by a leader who cannot articulate compelling ideas.

Ideas and **articulation skills** were the two basic pillars that empowered Islam to displace and replace Judaism and Christianity from their birth places, spread in people of color in Asia and Africa, in the centuries preceding the steam and electrical ages.

In order to nurture and advance those two critical assets (ideas and their articulation), Islam deviated greatly from Christianity in **banning liquor** from places of worship, banning paintings and statues from the same places, and emphasizing the ability and performance of the imam to convey ideas in Quranic feeling and content. In the absence of long and habitual consumption of liquor, many reciters of Quran kept fluid tongues, fluent articulation of vowels and consonants that suit the feeling of the complex verses of Quran.

There rose an art of **standardizing the articulation** of every verse, the locations and intensity of intervening stops, and the styles of resumption of articulation after numerous styles of interruption of flow of Quranic verses.

The few extreme ideas sought using musical equipments and singing Quranic verses, in the same manner used in Coptic churches, were immediately shunned. Sheikh Imam Issa rejected any tampering with the traditional vocalization of Quran and considered any farther musical composition tampering with the **divine nature of the holy verses**. Imam rejected the claim that singing the Quran aids it memorization or loosens it emotional appeal on people. Neither memorization nor appeal was intended for cursory learners or playful moods, as most Islamists perceive faith.

Essam Sultan, a modern Islamist attorney and heavy-weight intellectual of the Islamic Revolution, did not escape capture and imprisonment by the military coup of El-Sissi.

Sultan's deft integration of the heavenly canons of Islam with modern theories of civil laws made him a great menace to corruption and tyranny. Sultan presented paper evidence of bribed judges who sit high on the Egyptian judiciary appointed by Mubarak and conspired to impede the Islamic government. His famous proposal was drafting a law that **prohibits hypocrisy** by government officials. His drafted law prohibits posting the picture of the president in offices, naming schools, streets, or squares after presidents, dedicating long hours or pages in news outlets praising the president.

Sutlan's instantaneous wit and humor and his immediate integration of Quranic verses and canons of matters of law and politics made him a target for short-tempered military tyrants.

1.3. Institutionalized Corruption

In the wake of **industrial revolution**, European colonialists were able to invade every town, village, and island in the world, with large ships, trains, airplanes, and electronic communication. Therefore, the ancient life-style of self-sufficiency of villages, islands and oases gave way to government institutions. Remote communities became dependent on centralized governments for supplying equipments and raw materials and marketing agricultural and industrial products.

The war between **colonialists and nationalists** on controlling centralized governments dominated the African and Asian continents since the invention of the steam train in 1810 AD, until the end of WWII in 1945. Apparently, European colonialists entered two world wars in their competition to colonize the sources of food, fuel, and raw materials.

The weakening of European colonialists after two world wars led to liberation by anti-colonialists of many occupied nations. Those nationals succeeded in widening the gap between skillful Islamic orators, vocalists, and intellectuals, on one hand, and greater masses of illiterate, impoverished, and voiceless conscripts, on the other. The latter group was used efficiently to torture and kill the former group by Presidents Nasser, Sadat, Mubarak, and the present coup leader, **Abdul Fattah El-Sissi**.

Occasionally, **police conscripts** revolted, burned hotels, and expressed slight distress over high cost of living. That was swiftly controlled by the state. As the economic standards of Egypt fell below any bearable limit, millions of youths become unemployment and without future.

In contrast, few wealthy and connected officials flashed billions of dollars of properties and services. The masses faced the inevitable fate of getting together, not to throw out the government, but to seek **basic human rights** of food, jobs, shelter, education, and health care.

After thirty years of silencing voices of equality in Egypt, the 83-year old **Hosni Mubarak** has become too detached to keep tight control on many failing branches of the government.

In 1996, most security military officers in Cairo's Airport were not even supplied with proper uniforms that suit state officials. The traditional train and bus conductors, used to dress in government supplied uniforms, wore their own personal clothes. That reflects the extreme poverty of the branches of the government.

Amidst such bleak economic state, new **Egyptian billionaires** appeared and many of the state security police resorted to underground profitable crime activities.

The murder of the Lebanese pop star **Suzanne Tamim** in Dubai, in hire-to-kill by Egyptian billionaire and parliamentarian, **Hisham Talaat Mustafa** was the tip of the iceberg that would soon topple Mubarak's regime. Mustafa paid **Mohsen Al-Sukkari,** a National Security Officer, two million dollars to kill Tamim.

Mustafa Al-Sukkari (right) is on trial for the murder of Lebanese singer Suzanne Tamim (left). Hisham Talaat Mustafa (middle) paid Sukkari two million dollars to kill Tamim. Al-Sukkari killed Soad Hosni before but was not caught. He was an Egyptian National Security Officer, like many accused in killing thousands of civilian protesters during the revolution. Hisham Talaat Mustafa was a **billionaire by stealth** and corruption through his parliamentary position. Mubarak gave Talaat away due to the interference of foreign countries, Dubai and England, in the murder cases on their territories.

The murder of the famous actress **Soad Hosny** in London, England in 2001, on the hands of an Egyptian national security officer, was presented to the British Courts, as a case of suicide. British Prosecutors argued that a woman on the verge of suicide would not have been in the right state of mind to cut through steel netting. Hosny was thrown from a balcony to her death after reporting writing her diaries with **Abdulatif El-Menawy.**

Mohsen Al-Sukkari, who killed Suzanne Tamim, was later caught on a cell phone conversation in his second murder case in Dhabi, mentioning his role in the London's killing. Apparently, Al-Sukkari thought that his experience with the Egyptian National Security Police would help him evade forensic evidence. He was caught on video cameras before, during, and after the murder crime in Dhobi. El-Sukkari was even videoed taking a short relief on the boardwalk in front of the hotel where he slaughtered Tamim.

Those two crimes by the same hit man would have been considered casual incidents of homicide until we witness the **organized police killings** of civilians throughout the Egyptian Revolution against Mubarak's regime. The same organized killings occurred during the reverse revolution that brought Mubarak's men back to power. The crime would have been kept under the rug had not the governments of Dubai and Lebanon been involved in seeking the extradition of the killers to Dubai

The Egyptian Army Officer **Emad Salem** (left) made $1.5 million as an informant for the FBI in order to setup Sheikh **Omar Abdul-Rahman** (right) for court conviction and imprisonment. The Egyptian Army, Egyptian Police, and Egyptian National Security helped three tyrannical regimes to destroy Egypt and oppress its people. As the cost of living increased, those officers worked for hire-to-kill and as informants for profit.

In the above crime attributed to Sheikh Rahman, the informant Emad Salem was recorded on tape arguing with the FBI on how little the money sum he was paid to trap Rahman in terrorist plots.

Security Police Major General **Fouad Allam**, the son a police officer, whose father raised him on hatred and rejection of Muslim Brotherhood, grew up to haunt, arrest, fabricate charges against Muslim Brotherhood.

Prior to joining the Police force, Allam failed to join schools of engineering or medicine and was compelled to join the faculty of commerce, which he disliked. Later, Allam used **his father's connections** to join the police. On July 9, 2013, after the ousting of Morsi, Allam appeared on every TV channel allowed to broadcast by him and El-Sissi and launched naïve and lengthy campaign against islamists.

Allam's impulsive personality was apparent in his frequent cursing of islamists as "fools" and "ignorant". Allam claimed that the Brothers will burn the mosque of **Rabaa Al-Adawiya** to accuse the government for genocide. He also fabricated the claim that Muslim Brothers have heavy cannons and rockets on tops of buildings. He then arranged with Al-Arabiya, Misr AlHadas, to let a caller to call the TV station in the middle of the broadcast to claim that the caller saw with his own eyes boxes of ammunitions in the buildings surrounding Rabaa Al-Adawiya.

On August 14, 2014, the police and army executed the plot described by **Fouad Allam**.

Mustafa El-Fiqi, the Chairman of the Foreign Relations Committee at the People's Assembly attends a book signing ceremony of the director of the Mubarak Library **AbdAl-Raouf El-Reedy.** El-Fiqi served with Mubarak over twenty years and turned against him after he was kicked out in a sex-spy scandal involving General Abu Gazala and **Lucy Artin** using the two men to spy over Mubarak. **Lucy Artin** was a beautiful sexy business woman from an Armenian origin.

El-Fiqi was booted down by Muslim Brotherhood when he attempted to speak in Tahrir Square in front of revolutionary youth. The Muslim Brothers shouted at him: **"Baatel, baatel,..",** meaning "forbidden". El-Fiqi revealed many details on how Mubarak was an ignorant tyrant slipped gradually into delusion, and ended by losing grip on government. His constant theme, that Mubarak does not like any one to shine better than Mubarak and would act immediately to remove any new "star".

Mubarak threatened El-Fiqi that if he saw El-Fiqi's picture on **newspapers** or on magazines, he would not have any mercy in destroying El-Fiqi. When Mubarak travelled out of Egypt, General Tantawi made sure that no newspaper publishes Tantawi's photos on any magazine or paper, in order to avoid Mubarak's narcissistic ego.

A master of deception and corruption, El-Fiqi supported Mubarak in power, Morsi in power, and El-Sissi in power, but defamed all who lost power. An Egyptian peasant with many complex traits, El-Fiqi despised all those commented on his overweight and his morbid love for over eating. He described incidents of getting diarrhea and staying in bed for days. His frequent bragging about having his doctorate from Britain, his many successes to high academic positions, and his professorships in many prestigious universities is contrasted by his admission that Suzanne Mubarak asked him to sign his resignation for arriving late to her meeting. **El-Fiqi never protested being fired by a woman who does not hold any office and was not elected by the people.**

As a master snitch from Mubarak's deep state, El-Fiqi was rejected from presidency of the Assembly of the Arab Nations by Qatar and Sudan. Both described Fiqi as undesired man by people on the street. Fiqi claimed that a hundred people rallied on the streets for his support. When El-Sissi executed his coup against Morsi, Mustafa El-Fiqi did not hesitate to snitch to survive. El-Fiqi asserted that Egypt has no infra-structure for democratic processes and El-Sissi did the right thing. El-Fiqi then left the door open for future retreat by saying: "El-Sissi does not speak like Nasser, or Sadat, or any famous figure, but speaks casual in a family gathering".

Gamal Mubarak did not escape El-Fiqi's bitterness. Gamal fired **Osama Al-Baz,** the senior advisor to Mubarak, for correcting him during a visit to Washington.

Mustafa El-Fiqi owns the internal lexicon of hypocrite crooks. Those eased the path for Mubarak's thirty years of tyranny. Correcting the president in meeting or speeches signals the president to say: **"Do you want to govern Egypt instead of me?"** Alerting the president to improper appearance in a crowd agitated against him translates to suspicion that the advisor was part of agitating plot. **"Biz"** is a term that signified backstabbing from someone that would end the career of Mubarak's aides. **"Khazook"**, or wedge, meant that Mubarak decided to damage someone without known reasons.

Mubarak handed El-Fiqi the resignation papers of one of his aides and asked El-Fiqi to pass them to the aide in the middle of a meeting. The aide who was fired without reason, thanked Mubarak in front of the present crowd and explained that his rheumatoid arthritis was so severe that he was about to beg Mubarak for resignation.

In any case, El-Fiqi complained that Mubarak would think about an issue for two or three years before he credited any person for something good done by that person. In the end, Mubarak was surprised that he served his people for **thirty years** yet they still ask for more.

El-Fiqi expressed his shock that Mubarak was totally unaware that his people were impoverished beyond hope while Mubarak was enriched over his needs.

1.4. Sanctuary for Despots

The Arabian peninsula, the birth-place of Islam, earned the reputation of the sanctuary of every despot in Islamic nations. Even the people of Saudi Arabia describe the royal family of **Al Saud**'s family an implant forced upon them by the British colonialists, which do not represent Islamic values.

As will be seen in the Egyptian coup against Mohamed Morsi, Saudi Arabia was the first nation to support the illegal hijacking of democracy in Egypt.

Most Arabian treasures are stolen by kings, presidents and their agents and sent overseas. **Zine Al-Abidine Ben Ali**, the first head of Arabian state to be axed by the Arab Spring could not find a country to take him other than the kingdom of Saudi Arabia. The official Saudi Arabian news agency announced the arrival of Ben Ali on its territories soon after the public upheaval in Tunisia.

Thirty years earlier, General Aidi Amin was forced to flee into exile on April 11, 1979, settled later in Saudi Arabia. The Saudi royal family allowed him sanctuary and paid him a generous subsidy in return for his staying out of politics.

Arabian women in Saudi Arabia are banned from driving automobile or occupying many jobs that men occupy. In one of Mohammed Hassanien Heikal's interview on Al-Jazeera TV's The **Epic of Time**, Heikal depicts the scene of the sons of the King of Saudi Arabia rushing to the American operated oil company ARMCO, fighting for grabbing cash from the treasury of the company. Somehow, Saudi Arabia survived as the most authoritarian nation where few connected people took every thing for themselves. Saudi Monarchs oppress their people to the mindset of Dark Ages, before the rise of Islam.

The President of Uganda from 1971 to 1979, **General Idi Amin**, was ousted for political repression, ethnic persecution, extrajudicial killings, nepotism, corruption, and gross economic mismanagement. The Kingdom of Saudi Arabia was the natural place for his asylum.

20

Despite killing about 500,000, the King of Saudi Arabia received Amin and gave him asylum in Saudi Arabia. Unlike the American President **Jimmy Carter** who rejected the Shah of Iran, dumped him on Anwar Sadat of Egypt, the King of Saudi Arabia is described by most Saudis as a family brought to power by the British colonialists. Not that Jimmy Carter was nobler than the King of Arabia or the president of Egypt, but that Carter served the welfare of the United States. Allowing the Shah to live in the USA would have damaged its reputation by alienating the Iranian people. Those wanted to try the Shah for his crimes over 25 years.

Zein Abedeen Ben Ali enjoyed many decades of irresponsible plundering of Tunisia to the extent of total detachment from reality. As an ex-minister of interior, Ben Ali mastered the escape from being captured and tried in his own nation.

A man without heart always points to the wrong place. After his escape from Tunisia in the aftermath of burning of an unemployed citizen, Ben Ali's stolen wealth was estimated in billions. Some of the automobiles custom-manufactured with his name were too expensive to find a buyer in international auctions. **Ahmed Mansour** the reporter of Al-Jazeera TV channel and **Hassanien Heikal** carved a close picture to the rise and fall of Ben Ali.

Ben Ali finds no better friend than **George W. Bush**.

Both men were most disdained by their own people as well as by the international community.

Both men were forgotten as soon as their tenures ended, one by the force of revolution, the other by end or tenure. George W. Bush was fixed to the presidency by virtue of his father's connections. Due to his lack of any intellectual or literary achievements, Bush was unable to contribute to society and most probably reverted to alcohol addiction. Ben Ali was shut off public appearances due to his shameless crimes and theft.

This sign sums the twenty two years of the role of Ben Ali in plundering Tunisia.

Facing the grim reality of heavenly justice, Ben Ali lost his paranoid smile. Ben Ali led his people to impoverishment beyond hope, while he collected luxury cars, palaces, and enormous wealth stolen from people he governed.

The president of Tunisia, **Zein Abedeen Ben Ali,** was forced to abandon billions of stolen money spent on fancy cars, homes, and luxury palaces, grabbed whatever could fit in an airplane, and fled to any country that could accept him. The only nation that could afford a haunted despot was the Kingdom of Saudi Arabia and the birthplace of Islam.

In the far west of the ancient Islamic Empire, in Madrid, Spain, on June 17, 2011, Spanish judges set $38 million bail for a billionaire **Hussein K. Salem**, a friend of Hosni Mubarak. Salem was charged for money laundering, fraud, bribery and corruption related to the use of money that Mr. Salem is accused of obtaining illegally in Egypt.

Billionaire **Hussein Salem** is among many people who enriched themselves by exploiting three corrupt military regimes ruled Egypt between 1952 until 1911.

Salem left Egypt a week before Mr. Mubarak was forced to resign, put under house arrest in Egypt, expected to face trial on corruption and other charges. Salem was a major shareholder to buy gas from the government below market price and then resold the gas to Israel at a substantial markup, enriching himself at the public's expense. Salem provided Mubarak family with five luxury villas, including Mubarak's 161,000-square-foot seaside estate at **Sharm el Sheikh**.

1.5. State-Controlled Education

The introduction of state-controlled education in Egypt was inevitable phase in the history of a nation. After WWI, it became clear that the Ottoman Empire has slipped in technology. The western powers wasted no time in invading, grabbing, occupying the remains of the dying empire, and oppressing people with no access to technology.

The race for arms and militarization was the only hope for many nations to enable them to keep invaders from interfering with their fate. Modern physical sciences demand long and tedious education and training. Those offered better employment opportunities.

Thus, Islamic skills of memorization and vocalization of Quran, interpretation of Quranic verses and knowledge were deprived from the greatest intellectual minds. Those were diverted to the study medicine and engineering and other branches of science that grant higher social and economic status.

Among the newly bred Islamic technocrats, religious roots did not dry up. **Ayman Zawahiri** and **Sayyid Imam** were among those surgeons fought for Islamic justice against the tyranny of Sadat and Nasser.

In the confusion between secular physical sciences and Islamic Quranic interpretations, many new technocrats grasped the stark power of vocalization and figurative meaning of Quran. There is almost nothing in secular sciences that parallels Quranic treasures. Acting, singing, and impersonating characters rely solely of performance and talent of the actors but lack the targeted goal of administrating heavenly justice in society.

The schism between **humanitarian sciences** that serve feelings and sensation, and secular **physical sciences** that serve the material world, was not reconciled with the Quranic mix of law, justice, morality, and ability to vocalize their meaning to the people.

Sayyid Imam, a hard-wired surgeon and Salafi, wrote the manifesto of Jihad in Islam, never abandoned the concept of Jihad as the only way of establishing **Sharia Law**.

Sayyid Imam, the Egyptian surgeon from the generation of Ayman Al-Zawahiri and Al-Zawahiri's rival, viewed Deity as a working and living power, and disregarded reality altogether.

Imam (Imam is his name, not his title) fell in the trap of "God know. God does. God determines.", hence, his mission ended in vain, as did Ben Laden and Zawahiri.

To his credit, Sayyid Imam described Mohammed Morsi (who was still in power) and those who elected him as "Kafereen" or rebellions against Allah's heavenly canons.

سيد امام يكفر مرسي والمصريين اللي اخاتروه

Morsi fell few months after Sayyid Imam described him as "Kafer". Not because Imam has hand in it, but because Morsi picked what he liked from Quran, mixed it with what he liked from western secular openness, and forgot the dirty politics of **"survival for the fittest"**.

The most striking facts about the deep conviction of **Al-Zawahiri** and **Sayyid Imam** are that almost all their prophecies were proven valid over many decades. Al-Zawahiri and Imam fled Egypt to Afghanistan to escape execution. They succeeded in trapping the USA into the Iraq and Afghanistan quagmires, which ignited the Arab Spring and cascaded falling of most Arab tyrants.

Ben Ali	Ali Abdullah Saleh	Muammar Gaddafi	Hosni Mubarak
Fled	Expelled	Killed	Imprisoned
Tunisia	Yemen	Libya	Egypt

After **Saddam Hussein** was executed by Americans in December 30, 2006, it became clear that Arabs have failed miserably in cleansing their own homes. Since the rise of the Egyptian Revolution of 1952, Islamic Shia Iran chased the Shah out of power against the will of Super Power. Pakistan developed the atomic bomb, also against the will of Super Power. But Saddam enjoyed slaughtering his own people with impunity until that Super Power rooted his regime out of history. Sensing his inevitable fate and hoping to be left alone, **Muammar Qaddafi** surrendered his nuclear assets to the Americans. But, the turmoil in Tunisia ignited tsunamis of violence and unrest that swept the four despots out of power.

The spread of chaos enabled Sayyid Imam to return to Egypt during the brief reign of Mohamed Morsi, as did Mohamed Al-Zawahiri, the brother of Ayman Al-Zawahiri.

Sayyid Imam believed that all those who breached the heavenly canons of Allah are "Kafereen", including the one billion Indians or the greater number in China. Those do not do what Allah asked them to do, which is belief and work according to Quran.

In China and India, such formidable chaos of overpopulation diminished the human value into the lowest level of poverty. Values and heritage were all a poor human could possess not material luxury or even basic material needs.

In the Middle East, and particularly in Egypt, formidable chaos is vividly shown in one stark example in the University of Cairo. Forty thousand students were matriculated in 2013 in four colleges, while the country cannot create **jobs** for many millions of Egyptians. Meanwhile, connected Egyptians from the era before the 1952 revolution still have complete grip on the resources of the nation. Judges and academic professors are hired based on family ties. Those unconnected millions of Egyptians can only wish for the birth of another savior like **Gamal Abdul Nasser.** The alternative is resorting to riots, burning, and violence in order to gather greater momentum by encouraging silent people to join the fray.

1.6. Faith in Islam

In English language, faith conveys very limited ideas revolving around the concept of unquestionable and blind trust or belief without justification or reason.

In Islam, faith demands thorough inspection, inquisition, and justification. The clarity of ideas in Islam is always tied to the immediate **personal intents** of the imam than to the merits of Quranic verses. Since such manipulation of law, heavenly or human-made, is ubiquitous, not exclusive to Islamic cultures, the two fundamental powers of Quran (contents of verses and Quranic vocalization) empowered very diverse and vast population with Quranic knowledge. That created ongoing **Jihad** against corruption and injustice.

1.6.1. Pillars of Faith in Islam

(1) Faith that **Allah is the only God** that was not born, did not give birth, has no connection to anyone, and who existed from the beginning to eternity.

(2) Faith that Muhammad is the **servant of Allah** and **his messenger** to mankind.

Those two pillars are the most abused concepts by almost all those personnel tasked by administering the procedures of conversion to Islam to new converts.

Those two pillars of faith are stripped off their **philosophical content** and turned into contractual statements. Upon those statements, unwary converts must accept even without being given the length of time required to assimilate those philosophies or the reflection associated with reducing Islamic faith to the two statements.

In most instances of administering procedural conversion to Islam, the administering Imam comprises the weakest link and embarrassment to the **philosophy of Quran**. Because, neither the admission that "Allah is the only God" or that "Muhammad is God's servant and messenger" comprise any valid proof of faith of the new convert or even the born muslims.

On one hand, **personification of Allah** in the image of a God, that does or does not commit actions, renders the concept of Allah an earthly matter that seeks earthly characterization. The recognition of Allah by exclusion is also daunting and leads to the same end, that Allah is a supreme concept that exceeds our ability to describe beyond doubt.

That is not an **exceptional challenge** to man since we face endless challenges to which we have no answers.

We lack any **deterministic power** on the choice of our parents, gender, time or place of birth, or course of development and evolution. True that we could plan many things ahead of time and carry them through, but those things are limited to our temporal limits and physical power.

We cannot travel or live outside the solar system because our age limit defeats such undertaking. We cannot probe or visualize subatomic events because our sensual instruments are limited to our scientific achievements. Those are mostly accidental, rather than deterministic. Even mundane events; marriage, employment, or adhering to safe or sound styles of living are controlled by **divine interventions** in all aspects.

Even though Quran is **spoken in the words of Allah**, the philosophy of attributing written canons to the person of Allah could only be explained as **universal canons** to which mankind should conform. Because, all humans share the striking unison of mental shrewdness, functions, ability to infer, and inclination to react in unified and predictable fashion in response to specific ideas.

How did Muhammad reach the universal canons attributed to Allah?
Why should billions of people trust Muhammad for writing the first Islamic legislature without any possible objective link to a conceptual God?

Those are the hard-core criticisms directed to Islam by most secular or even muslims with clear and objective analysis of causes and effects.

Prophet Muhammad relied on the exact logic of discerning the **meaning of the creator** from the acts of creation.

Therefore, those early associates of Muhammad, who lived and felt the meanings of the Quranic verses were captivated by the unprecedented **rationale of the verses** and sensed the immediate implications of preserving and spreading Quran.

Muhammad's associates: Abu Baker, Omar Ben Khattab, Osman Ben Affan, and Ali Ben Abu Taleb, all felt the potential of growth in power had Muhammad's Quran was disseminated to new people outside the Arabian Peninsula.

Thus, Muhammad's credibility was tested on the ground of greater expansion in new cultures across the globe. The **consensus** of the new converts to Islam would be the only answer given to whether Muhammad's heavenly canons deserve such characterization.

Muhammad's canons would have perished without the conviction of his associates with the viability of Quran and the practicality of implementing Islamic canons in different cultures.

1.6.2. Rewards and Punishment

Islam spread on the two pillars of faith; **Allah and Muhammad**.

Those must transcend cultures conveying the message that people are equal in front of supreme creator. The creator is not human, has no relatives or preferred associates, only good deeds give passage to **God's paradise: Heaven.**

There goes another complex concept of **rewards and punishment**; heavens and hell.

Even though many interpreters of Quranic verses adhere to the immediate literal meaning of words, the concepts of **heavens and hell** cannot be different from the ubiquitous and well recognized concepts of intuition, inference, association, and ingenuity. Those are universal and predicable abilities in humans to initiate, invent, and plan.

Hence, heavens and hell lose their space and time features and occupy greater domain in our conscience.

That some human minds exemplify **heavens**, some exemplify **hell** is easily discernable by watching the extreme spectrum of people's ability to construct and enrich life. One cannot dismiss the fact that some people are blessed with clear and straight logic that leads to clear and realistic outcome, some do not, and some lay between the two.

The credibility of Islam is rooted in its ability to simplify the figurative canons of Quran such that the rewards and punishments are justly assigned to good and bad deeds, upholding a unique and simple concept of **"Allah Is Great"**. That signifies the greater purpose of mankind united in such concept of one God of unified canons that places man in his right place in the universe.

Over fourteen centuries, Islam succeeded in captivating the minds of billions of followers around the concept that "Allah Is Great" signifying that every person looks up to **the same canons of the universe devised by its creator.**

1.6.3. Unison in Nature
The **unification of human purpose** in the universe received greater support from the world of physical sciences. In the Christian cradle of modern sciences of Europe, the dispute over the human nature of Jesus or the heavenly powers of the church led to discovering the fundamental laws of nature. Those contradict all claims made by church.

Neither biology nor physics supported the concept that religious powers could breach the **laws of material world**. The progress in material sciences faced the impasse of origin of matter and energy. That led to the greater impasse of the rise of life within the same domain of matter and energy.

Yet, there are indisputable **unified laws** that govern matter and energy, some of which were revealed and affirmed by men, some remain mysterious. As did Prophet Muhammad in proposing the concept of one God and unified heavenly laws of Quran, physical scientists became unified on the concept of one origin of matter and energy; some proved that matter could be created from energy, and vice versa.

As basic sciences tackled common practical physical problems, invention of machines and means of communication followed. Yet, many **scientific fields remain prohibited** on man due to either space limitations or time limitations that exceed man's ability to overcome.

Man overcame the space limitation of micrometer and nanometers by inventing optical and electronic microscopes. Those enabled man to navigate in such tight and narrow spaces within matter. But, **celestial space** might not be conquered or even needed to be conquered by man due to its extreme vastness and emptiness.

Similarly, man managed to perform operations at the femato second level but hindered on the time scale exceeding light years or even closer to that. On both fronts of space and time, and equally on both fronts of figurative heavenly canons and physical scientific canons, man is grasping the inevitable fact of **set limits**. In both objective materialism and figurative spiritualism, limits are set clear such that man must live according to his intellectual and physical means. Those are neither unlimited nor well–defined on personal level. They can only be discerned by consensus rather than by individually defined criteria.

1.7. The Rituals of Orderly Living

In **Sunni Islam**, there are perceived five rituals or pillars that a muslim is encouraged to adhere to as basic necessities of faith. They are:

Oath (Shahadah):	declaring there is no god except God, and Muhammad is God's servant and messenger
Prayer (Salat):	ritual prayers, five times a day
Fasting (Sawm):	fasting and self-control during the blessed lunar month of Ramadan
Charity (Zakat):	giving portion of one's earnings to the poor and needy
Pilgrimage (Hajj)	Hajj to Mecca at least once in a lifetime for able maslims.

The five pillars are divided such that:

The oath determines individual intent.
The prayers remind the person to cease daily activity and ponder about the purpose of life.
Fasting tie the hungry with needy who cannot afford eating, and disciplines one's desires.
Charity confers sense of belonging to herd.
Pilgrimage expands the size of the herd from local town to greater nations.

1.7.1. Oath or Shahada

Shahada is directed to the conscience of the person.

"I bear witness that there is none worthy of worship except God and Muhammad is His Servant and Messenger."

Reciting this statement is obligatory or desirable in a person's conversion to Islam.

The brilliance of Islam is distilling its ingredients to those concise **declarative statements** that could be repeated at the opening of any speech, dialogue, daily interaction, or praying.

Thus, a muslim could recite the oath at the beginning of all events or talking, such as upon eating, upon waking up, upon going to be, upon starting study, or upon praying. That translated to wrapping every thing in life by **vocalized contractual oath** that there is no God but Allah and that Muhammad is his servant and messenger.

In the event of confronting something irrational, evil, destructive, or damaging, the muslim could raise the tone of the oath so as to declare to the defaulting person that he or she is deviating from God's **straight path**.

Farther reduction of the complexity of Islam implies that a person, who recites the oath or Shahada, in good faith, is considered among the forgiven in front of God.

The essence of such canon is very vivid in the fact that the vast majority of people experience stunning sense of guilt or rigidity in moments when they should reverse the tide of anger and aggression. Many resent verbalizing declarative admission that God is above all our trivial obsessions. Not a personified God, but God in the sense of **purpose** and **cause** for existence.

Should a man kill or hurt another man for wrong doing?
Or, would a man commit such extreme acts if he or she recited the oath (Shahada) before engaging in killing or hurting others?

Should a man damage a tree or hurt an animal?
Or, would a man engage in such mundane acts if he or she recited the oath (shahada) before engaging in those casual deeds?

Hence, shahada raises the **conscience** of conflicts to the real context in relation to the canons of the supreme creator.

1.7.2. Prayer or Salat

Praying is directed to daily **routine** and behavior of the person.

Friday's group prayer at noon comprises a weekly gathering that impose greater force on unjust rulers or great calm on acceptable ruling.

Salat (Ṣalāh) is the Islamic prayer. It consists of five daily prayers according to Sunna branch of Islam.

Those are given names according to the time of prayer:

Fajr (dawn), Duhr (noon), Asr (afternoon), Maghrib (evening), and Isha' (night).

Fajr prayer is performed before sunrise.
Duhr is performed in the midday after the sun has surpassed its highest point.
Asr is the evening prayer before sunset.
Maghrib is the evening prayer after sunset.

Isha is the night prayer.

Prayers are performed with the person facing in the direction of the **Kaaba** in Mecca of Saudi Arabia. Muslims living in various parts of the world have various means of determining the direction to face in prayer. To avoid the argument of spherical globe, direction is assumed based on surface travel. Thus, a muslim in Indonesia faces west and slightly north. A muslim in Britain faces east, and slightly south.

The direction of face during praying carries no reflection on the geographic location of Mecca. It only amounts to agreeing on **unity in rituals** with all muslims.

Muslim prayers must wash before prayer. This is called **wudu** or "purification". Prayers' washing take place prior to each of the five daily prayers follows a protocol.

If the prayer was cleansed wholly priory, then **prayer's washing** is limited to limbs distal to elbows and knees, mouth, nose, face, hair, ears, and neck. Those parts are cleansed by water in three paths each. Cleaning with sand was allowed in situations where water cannot be accessed or in time of war and places where sand is available.

If prayer **moved bowel or urine**, then those places have to be cleansed before prayer's washing is contemplated.

If prayer was **not bathed wholly** and that internal parts of the body were not cleansed, then total body bath should be contemplated before prayer's washing is contemplated.

The prayer is accompanied by a series of set positions including:
(1) Standing and reading few verses from Quran.
(2) Bowing with hands on knees and reading oath while in the fully forward bent position.
(3) Prostrating (sitting on knees and toes, bringing forehead on the ground face downward) and reading verses from the Quran.
(4) Sitting in a special position (not on the heels, nor on the buttocks, but on knees and toes) and reading verses from the Quran.

The transitions between the above four positions and the number of full cycle of positions requires another reference on praying.

In short, Islamic prayers manage the daily hours onto five segments depending on the position of the sun in the sky into rituals of bodily cleaning, seclusion, meditation, and recitations of few versus of the Quran. The five daily intermissions remind the muslim to **stop and ponder** five times daily on the purpose of life, creation, and God.

The first president in the Islamic History who led audience in prayers, Mohamed Morsi mastered the Quranic canons and the means to communicate them in real life. Note the ability of Morsi to sit on his lower legs in such age, when no western man could do the same in such stage of life. Sitting and praying in such keeling position on daily basis led to such state of flexibility.

Secular TV commentator Amr Adeeb criticized Mohamed Morsi for leading prayers when he was suppose to **lead a nation**. Adeeb, who was educated in Britain and speaks and thinks like Hashish-addicts on the streets of urban Egypt, Adeeb could not sense the immense power of leading people in prayers, speaking, thinking, and delivering Islamic speeches.

Even though photographing a praying muslim is viewed as sign of hypocrisy and trade in religion, faith, and God, Mohamed Morsi was well-known for his resentment to taking decisive changes. Being from Sharqia providence of Egypt, known for its docile and hospitable inhabitants, Mohamed Morsi could have not sensed the impropriety of photographing him praying. He most probably assumed being a good model for children. Or, that his photograph was taken by unmanned camera. Thus, the photographer was not prevented from praying with the prayers for the sake of **marketing a faithful president**.

An unfaithful marketing photographer should not be working with a **faithful president**. The common man would assume.

1.7.3. Fasting or Sawm

Fasting is directed to disciplining bodily desires.

Fasting from food, drink, or any **oral intake**, is an obligatory act during the month of Ramadan. Muslims must abstain from food and drink, from dawn to dusk during this month, and are to be especially mindful of other gratifications such as sexual practices, gambling, foul talking, or any negative acts that do harm and do no good.

34

Fasting is necessary for every muslim that has reached puberty. Exceptions are made for medical conditions that can be aggravated by fasting. Those must be identified by a muslim doctor, not by an antagonistic to Islam.

Some muslims might still adhere to the traditional break of their fasts in the month of Ramadan with dates as practiced by Muhammad. (We will not deal with the types of fasting in this book. We also will not delve into the many purposes of fasting but emphasize the strict discipline it imposes upon the person.)

Weaning the digestive track from food for sixteen hours increases the awareness of the person of the potentials and limitations of the body in managing energy and work.

1.7.4. Charity or Zakāt
Donation or charity or zakat is directed towards living in community.

Giving alms to those in hardship is an obligatory charitable practice on all muslims who are able to do so. It is not meant to encourage unaccountable **indifference to earning living with honor**; neither has it applied to wealth obtained by illegal means.

In modern Islamic nations where corruption is pervasive, the present application of zakat by illegally enriched people is a **distortion of Islam**. When people cannot gain equal opportunities for employments, while few are in control of the fate of a nation, greater issues of justice must be addressed before stolen wealth is partitioned unfairly between improperly enriched and severely impoverished majority.

On individual scale, little donation by able people could change the outcome for those in hardship in the immediate family or neighborhood. Hence, the religious canon helps nuclear families to administer justice away from state politics.

1.7.5. Pilgrimage to Mecca or Hajj

Hajj or Pilgrimage is directed to unite diverse races and remote peoples, in one location and time every year.

Hajj takes place during the Islamic or lunar month of Zu Al-Hijjah. It comprises travel to the holy city of Mecca in Saudi Arabia. Every able muslim is obliged to make the pilgrimage to Mecca at least once in their life. The rituals of Hajj are left to other references to describe.

Among the unforeseen aspects of Hijj can be told through stories like **Malcolm-X**'s. As an American black isolated from the outside world, Malcolm-X was treated by white Americans as an inferior man of color. In that era in the United States, many states in the United States segregated blacks from white in living, schools, and public facilities.

Muhammad Ali (right) and Malcolm-X (left) might not have grasped much of Quran, but both men walked away with the single most fundamental law of nature: **Allah Is Great**. What does it mean? It meant black people are no different from white people. That a supreme God created the most intelligent and ingenious human beings in the same manner the whole universe was created. That the gift of the color of the skin was erroneously construed by flawed minds. **Muhammad is his servant and messenger** meant that the illiterate and poor prophet Muhammad is the sole legislator of the laws by which the two men should live.

Muhammad Ali refused to fight the Vietnamese because they were people of yellow color and poor, and thus share the same enemy in the white man. Ali conceived white Americans as his enemy because they alone treated him as an inferior human being.

On his way to Mecca and on land, Malcolm-X could not believe that people from all corners of the world treated him as equal. He returned to America changed man, with grand scope on Islam far different from his obstructed views that his battle was against white discrimination. Malcolm-X sensed that the power of Islam was much greater than the bitterness toward people entrapped in superficial culture of physical attraction.

CHAPTER 2

Fiction in the Practice of Islam

2.1. Literal Mystification of Quranic Ideas

2.1.1. Coptic Mystification of the Divine

Quranic verses are taught in early childhood and mostly by sheikhs, imams, or teachers. Those must accommodate the young age of the learner by reducing complex philosophical issues to their **literal** meanings. That afforded the mentor chance to cover vast contents of Quran in reasonable period of time.

Many followers of Islam make the serious errors made by Christians. Those interpret Jesus as a supernatural magician who can heal the sick, bring sight to the blind, walk on water, or convert water to wine.

Even in this modern age, in Egypt, and on the Arabiya.net famous TV program "The Egyptian Event" by Mahmoud El-Warwary, a prominent Egyptian intellectual Copt claimed that the **Bethlehem of Galilee** in Jerusalem, Palestine, has an ongoing miracle since the birth of Jesus. Copts view the candles of Bethlehem powered by the Holy Spirit. Modern Egyptian history is filled with stories about Copts gathering in Cairo to witness the appearance of Holy Mary in the skies of Cairo.

The Christian magic has long sentenced **Christianity** into disfavor among civilized nations. Yet, Egyptian Christianity is even more extreme on magic, indulgence on singing, touching, liquor, and physical rituals that have nothing to do with refining articulation of language or expanding the repertoire of ideas and problem solving.

In fact, no one in Christianity claims that Jesus wrote the Bible, even though muslims believe that the Bible was sent from God on Jesus, and the Torah on Moses. Yet, Christians believe that the Bible was written by apostles inspired through the Holy Spirit. Thus, Jesus' human participation in writing the Bible is totally illogically.

Such chasm between Christianity and Islam made Quran inherently a **political textbook** beside its moral and spiritual weight.

In Egypt, the Islamic government is an inevitable course of history in the view of long and brutal injustice practiced by secular governments. Soon after the ousting of Mohamed Morsi, El-Sissi was able to use the **judicial system** to imprison fifteen thousands islamists, including the elected president Mohamed Morsi. El-Sissi was aided by judges appointed by Mubarak's regime.

The tradition of Judges appointing their children to same positions, university professors appointing their children to same positions, and police and military officers doing the same, has been practiced in Egypt, mostly before the Ottoman invasion of Egypt in 1517 A.D.

2.1.2. Al-Azhar's Mystification of the Divine

One such prominent fallacy adopted and contended by many hard-core literal interpreters of Quran is whether Prophet Muhammad ascended physically to Heaven from **Masjid Aqsa** versus being a revelation of mental dimensions, not physical transportation.

Even though Islam prohibits magic and superstition, yet many interpreters of Quran claim that Prophet Muhammad had the privilege to breach the laws of nature and ascend to Allah. That is among many skirmishes between Sunni and Shia regarding the people of the house of Mohammed.

Muhammad Husayn Haykal is one among those who advocated the above literal interpretation is in his book "The Life of Muhammad", published in 1933. Haykal was an Egyptian writer, journalist, politician and Minister of Education of Egypt. The author tackled three disputed claims by Christians, regarding the merits of Islam, in such fictional manner that defeats the reason and logic in Islam.

Haykal claimed that the appearance of **Angel Gabriel** to Prophet Muhammad was a physical occurrence that entailed the arrival of a physical entity from Allah to inspire Muhammad. Haykal then suggested that electromagnetic waves travel as the speed of light; therefore the Holy Prophet should not be denied the power of Allah who could enable Muhammad to travel to Heaven at any speed determined by Allah.

Haykal made the third gross error of affirming that Muhammad **married under-aged wife**. Haykal equated that by similar privilege given to Jesus of being born without sexual impregnation of a female by male.

Haykal's forcible manipulation and distortion of Islamic philosophy is one among many distortions made by people with good-will who could not grasp the universal and ancient superiority of man's intellect. This needs no physical **flying angels** to inspire a prophet to produce unique work of Quran.

No doubt that Haykal cannot claim to be a physics expert in electromagnetic angels or possess undisputed birth or marital documents from Muhammad's generation or even could affirm or deny the creation of Jesus without a father. Equally, **Haykal**'s fictional interpretation tainted muslim thinkers with such close-mindedness and irrational analysis of matters beyond their ability to comprehend.

Haykal's attempts to balance Islam against Christianity, conferring **magical traits** on Prophet Muhammad equal to those conferred on Jesus, permitting Muhammad to travel to heavens and see God in the manner which Christians view Jesus, or the manner that Shia muslims view the twelve Imams, were **new inventions** lacking any merit in the history of Islam.

Prophet Muhammad adhered to consistent logic, declared that he was a human and messenger, like many messengers before him.

Muhammad's Islam never sanctioned any magical traits attributed to Muhammad. In fact, the burial of muslims in **unmarked graves** is an ancient held tradition, which prohibits glorifying the dead. Islam emphasizes the value of the deeds of the person, not his or her personification.

Hence, Salafi muslims demolished the statues of **Buddha in Afghanistan** and suggested the demolition of the Pyramids. They view those as idols worshipped by westerners and visitors.

Regardless of the immense historical significance of ancient ruins, Salafi muslims have always been ingenious and transparent regarding the **apathy of civilized nations** to the human suffering and promoting classes of few elites over classes of impoverished and voiceless majority.

Those seeking the demolition of the Pyramids watch wealthy foreigners arrive to view the Pyramids and marvel at their **glory** with total apathy towards the poorest human population living on the hills of the Pyramids.

Haykal's compromising stances from the 1930's were farther enhanced by Nasser's revolution and Nasser's brutal oppression of islamists. Hence, a more abusive Orthodox Christianity flourished in Egypt amounting to state-sponsored dissemination of superstitious teachings.

2.1.3. Shia's Mystification of the Divine

On the sectarian level, warring Sunni and Shia muslims fight over the Shia's mystification of Imams as waiting souls with futuristic characteristics that breach all laws of nature. Shia go to the extreme to insult and demean the associates of Prophet Muhammad on an ancient dispute over the Caliphate of **Ali Ben Abu Taleb**, the nephew of Prophet Muhammad and the first Islamic convert among Koraish.

Recently, during the upheaval in Syria, Imam **Muqtada Sader** issued fatwa vindicating the Sunni muslims from the blood of Hussein, a historic incident from the remote centuries. Thus, Sader did not attempt to uplift his own Shia followers above the bittiness of distracting issues that do not even relate to the spiritual purpose of faith. Sader aimed at keeping his crowd under his control, which might help him in future wars, when controlling illiterate followers determine the outcome of bloody battles.

Fictional and superstitious twisting of Quranic verses to suit the Shia's mindset is equally encountered by the most corrupt, tyrannical, and obsolete **Sunni's governing bodies**. Shias succeeded in toppling the Shah after brutal oppression that lasted between 1951 and 1978, with triumphant erection of the first Islamic government in the twentieth century.

Immediately, the Iranian Islamic Revolution was attacked by Sunni's regimes, aiding and abetting **Saddam Hussein**'s eight-year war against Iran. In the end, Iran recovered, started a nuclear program and manufactured its own weapons, while the wealthy Arab Monarchs spared no time plundering their people and enriching themselves.

Comparing the newly elected Egyptian Sunni leader Mohamed Morsi with the Iranian Shia Khomeini, Morsi's academic preparation as an engineering professor could not compete with **Ayatallah Khomeini.** The latter was fully-fledged imam with stern conviction in the words of God.

Mohamed Morsi was easily ambushed by lesser military officer, Abdul Fattah El-Sissi. This was supported by the same powers that pushed Saddam to derail Khomeini's revolution. The **Kings of Saudi Arabia**, who paid Saddam to wage war against Iran, urged George W. Bush to remove Saddam Hussein.

2.1.4. Laymen's Skepticism of the Mystification of the Divine

The greater power of oppressed, hopeless millions of Egyptians reached critical mass of anger, soon after the 1967's war.

In 1971, Anwar Sadat felt the stampede of angry Egyptians unwilling to allow military men to plunder Egypt. Sadat was given no chance but to fight Israel or lose his life. Sadat did both, fought Israel in 1973 and was assassinated in 1981, by **Jihad islamists**.

Among those released in Sadat's murder case, many insisted that Sadat was rightfully executed for breaching all canons of heavens.

Ahmed Fouad Negm, the rebellious Egyptian poet wrote and sang poems praising Khalid Islamboullie, who assassinated Sadat, described Sadat as an imposter and sick man, Nasser as a prophet of his time made from the pride and decency of poor Egyptians.

Ahmed Fouad Negm was an orphaned child from the poorest Egyptian peasants and the subject of this author's two books that introduced Negm's work to the west. Negm won 2013 Prince Claus Award for '**Unwavering Integrity**'. Negm climbed to fame on the pillars of Quranic vocalization and endless riches. Those were mastered by the blind composer and singer Sheikh Imam Issa.

Negm sensed the immense power of Quran on the eloquent and beautiful voices of Imam Issa. Imam lifted Negm's star to fame from 1962 through 1995. Imam died from complications of diabetes. Negm is publically known as a marihuana addict, self-educated, always been oppressed, beaten, tortured, and imprisoned by Nasser, Sadat, and Mubarak's regimes. Negm lost every right or privilege in Egypt until the three presidents were either dead, killed, or imprisoned.

Even though Negm was attacked by Muslim Brothers as a pot-smoker and Kafer, Negm's exceptional talent in poetry and his stubborn and steadfast Jihad against major heads of state and tyrants distinguished the slim and poor poet in his generation.

Negm's words were clear and final verdicts against despots and dictators rooted in the extreme injustice inflicted on Negm by almost all figures of authority. His uncles robbed his mother from her inheritance. In orphanage, he was neglected in any education. The Egyptian governments haunted him, imprisoned him for eighteen years for speaking the truth.

Negm's brilliance could not be dismissed even though it throws islamists into epileptic fits. Negm believes that the Egyptian were the first people looked to the skies and determined that there must be a creator. Thus, Negm's idea that **God was created by the Egyptians** has skipped the minds of many simple minded islamists.

Negm concluded that Egypt must be put above Islam, not under it. Even though Negm succeeded almost every time he tackled a conflict, his prophecies lack the mechanism of action that could account for the global realities of major powers. In fact, Negm's puritanical views that governments should be noble and conscientious bodies that serve the people cost Negm his reputation and kept people at bay from his impractical views.

Negm sat on Christian TV shows to attack islamists, appease Christians, unaware of the hidden agendas and foreign powers of those Christian agents. Negm did the same with secular TV stations, funded and supported by all his oppressors of the past three presidential regimes. Negm's dire need for money in his late age softened his stance and made him a tool in the hands of secular propaganda media.

Negm's star dimmed soon after the death of sheikh Imam Issa in 1995. But, the new star of **Mohamed Fawzy Bakous** was born.

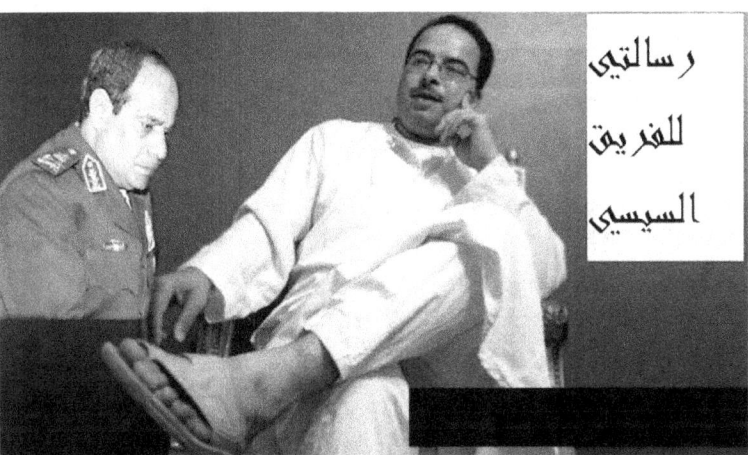

Mohamed Fawzy Bakous (nick-named after the town of Bakous, where Nasser and this author were also born) is a free-lance comedian with acute sense of humor, immediately representing millions of voiceless Egyptians. On the Seventh Day newspaper, under the title "**Campaign to bring down the next president**", Bakous predicted the ousting of Mohamed Morsi before Morsi was elected.

After El-Sissi entertained the idea of running for presidency, Bakous reminded him that those who mentioned Generals Eisenhower and de Gaulle should have also mentioned Hitler and Mussolini. The latter two were military officers who destroyed their nations.

Bakous then threw **Winston Churchill** on El-Sissi to show that the man who won WWII against Hitler was rejected by the Britain to rule during peace time. Bakous counted the achievements of Churchill, a fraction of which El-Sissi cannot even dream to accomplish.

Despite Bakous's limited education of associate diploma in electronics, he reminded El-Sissi that the thirty four Egyptian TV stations he permitted to run were fooling him. Bakous described them all running in one direction on the same highway, in the same way they fooled Mubarak.

The impact of Quranic verses on Mohamed Bakous is vividly illustrated in a casual statement he made to Al-Jazeera TV, in which he said:

"Right is the name of Allah and no matter how long or how much it takes, Allah is the greatest and right must prevail."

We are therefore confronted by few diverse **styles of mystification** of Quranic verses.

(1) Those **career-professionals** making living under the banner of religious authorities such as Haykal, Ghoneim, and Sader. They advocate what people wish to hear despite the clear breach of cause and effect in mystification.

(2) Those **freelance artists** such as Ahmed Fouad Negm and Mohamed Fawzy Bakous. Those could reach crystal clear understanding of purpose of faith, yet lack the shrewdness of planning to ward off the intrusion of more serious mystification of secular decay, social ills of alcohols, drugs, prostitution, enslavement of the poor, and unjust and free plundering of nation by immoral secular leaders.

In fact, Negm and millions of unwary Egyptians were robbed, oppressed, and cheated of any civilized living or future by the secular, immoral opportunists. Those enriched themselves at the expense of the people they governed.

(3) The third style of mystification of the Quranic verses belongs to the Islamic sects, each with its own views on how the words of God should become government policy. **Salafi muslims** see nothing less than adopting the Islamic Sharia and strictly adhering to the justice and system of governing of Prophet Muhammad and his immediate associates. In such realm, Islam breaches all geographical boundaries and engulfs unprecedented races, nationalities, and localities competing to implement utopian justice for the poor.

(4) The moderate and practical realization of Quranic verses adopted by **Muslim Brotherhood** imposes serious threat to most wealthy monarchs and hundreds of thousands of Egyptians who inherited wealth grabbed from the era of Ottoman regime in Egypt. Most of the latter group weathered well during Nasser's attempts to nationalize Egyptian industries, limit ownership of agricultural land to families, and enable impoverished peasants to own the land they farm.

After Nasser's death, Sadat reversed all accomplishments made by Nasser and started the present state of chaos and anarchy. The efforts of the Muslim Brothers to purge the Egyptian government from the deep and imbedded agents of Mubarak's and Sadat's regime collided by the realities of anarchy and chaos left over from Mubarak's total negligence of managing the ailing and bankrupt state. Hence, Muslim Brothers faced the inevitable outcome of failure in face of well-armed military thrived on plundering Egypt for sixty years.

(5) The last and most morbid mystification of Quranic verses belongs the **secular and Coptic class of Egyptians**, raised and educated in western institutions and grown up fascinated with the materialistic success of western societies. Most of those mix foreign words with Arabic words in most sentences and are entirely hostile to Quranic teachings. Those declare their beliefs that Muhammad was a just and good man of his time, but their time is theirs alone to set their own moral, economic, and political agendas.

2.1.5. Western Mystification of the Divine

This latter style of mystification of Quranic verses was not only a product of the western influence of introducing fields of studies that demean Islam and Quran. Westerners equate the two with the defunct **Christian doctrines** that elevated the Pope to the status of God.

On March 1208, **Pope Innocent** of Catholic Church in Rome placed an **interdict** on England, prohibiting clergy from conducting religious services, with the exception of baptisms for the young, and confessions and absolutions for the dying.

King John of England treated the interdict as the equivalent of a "**papal declaration of war**". King John seized the lands of those clergy unwilling to conduct services, as well as those estates linked to Innocent himself; and promised protection for those clergy willing to remain loyal to him.

The example of a Pope from **Rome**, Italy, manipulating the affairs of people in **England**, did not include supporting the poor, caring for the sick, or educating the illiterate. Merely, the Catholic Pope appointed the clergies who could collect crops, money, and property from people as a price for his Christian blessing and endorsement.

The Islamic movements throughout history rejected the concept of empowering men to manipulate others under the name of God.

In those bred and educated in **resenting religion** in general and Islam in particular, the main thrust of their logic is the close mind of religious thinkers and followers and their detachment from the realities of business, compromise, and invention.

Those legitimate and appealing reasons for rejecting religious doctrines have been tested and rejected categorically by millions of Egyptians. Those lived, learned about, and studied the ruthless class struggle in secular societies and the long and consistent brutality of Mubarak, Sadat, and Nasser's associates.

Mubarak's justified the wealth of his two sons by their work outside Egypt when he was the president of Egypt for thirty years. Not only that **Mubarak's sons** used the power of the state to gain power outside Egypt, but that Mubarak acknowledges his inability to afford his own sons the chance to live and work in Egypt like the people governed by the father, Hosni Mubarak.

As **Mustafa Al-Bakry** explained, Mubarak believed and acted to get permission from George W. Bush to enable Gamal Mubarak to inherit the Egyptian presidency. Mubarak played on the card of containing Islamic terrorism from 1981 until his ousting in 2011.

As Mubarak aged, his **security apparatus** split between those enriching themselves by embezzlement and corruption and those foot-soldiers living under the line of poverty and lacking even the basic literacy required to training and enforcing law. Millions of hungry and unemployed youths flooded the streets. Mubarak's cronies succeeded in tranquilizing the masses by the hope of democratic process in order to return, reverse the revolution and practice the same game of containing terrorism.

Amr Adeeb mastered the western clowns of selling false and fabricated facts to tread in his country. Adeeb is impressed by the American TV host **Jay Leno**'s collection of 70 expensive cars and the wealth he accumulated through his TV career.

Adeeb's TV has never generated any revenues that justify what people claim his salary of 20 million dollars per year. Yet, **many of the billionaires** who grabbed vast wealth since Sadat's era fund demagogues like Adeeb, in support for secular Egypt. Adeeb speaks in the dialect of hashish and opiate addicts, inhabiting many cafés scattered in urban centers in Egypt.

Dialect alone, in the Arabian and Islamic cultures, suffice discredit the speaker who cannot adhere to the spirit of Islam. Quiet, logical, and moral contents of a speech must conform to the figurative canons of Quran, which Adeeb lacks.

While in Washington DC to meet Senator McCain, Adeeb ran into a **Harvard graduate Egyptian** who impressed Adeeb with his critics of El-Sissi's coup. The Harvard graduate pointed to Adeeb that Muslim Brothers in prisons and military people in power comprise a shock to Americans who dread military ruling. Adeeb returned to Egypt advising Egyptians that sending their kids to Harvard and European schools was the best investment in brightening brain centers beyond what Egyptians can do at home.

Amr Adeeb forgot that **Enron's scandal** was committed by graduates from Yale and Harvard universities, and that George W. Bush graduated from both Ivy League schools. Yet, Bush could not write, speak, or think as sane people could. George W. Bush joined both schools because of his father's status, not his intellect.

Adeeb's fascination with western decay and his impoverished knowledge of Islam and Quran were the exact reasons that led Gamal Mubarak to prison.

As **Mustafa El-Fiqi** stated, Gamal Mubarak focused on America and Europe, never paid attention to Arab nations, African nations, internal affairs, or extremely marginalized Egyptians. Those rendered Gamal Mubarak a foreign transplant in the Egyptian body that must be rejected. Gamal Mubarak flashed the book of Quran as soon as was dressed in prison uniform, not before.

Adeeb interviews the Egyptian Major General **Ahmed Wasfy**, of the Second Army on the Suez Canal. Ahmed Wasfy claims that Allah loves Egypt and mentioned it 13 times in Torah, 5 times in Quran, and blessed its people of the Bible. Wasfy concluded that that suffices protect Egypt.

This is an example of the Egyptian military officers now leading Egypt to total chaos. Amr Adeeb asks the fat Ahmed Wasfy if he sleeps it night. How long could a fat person work or produce in any profession?

Ahmed Wasfy claimed that because Allah promised to keep Egypt safe, even **Iblis** cannot hurt Egypt if Iblis wishes. But Israel did worse than Iblis and El-Sissi killed thousands and imprisoned over 15,000 Islamists. (Iblis is a ghost figure in Quran that exemplifies wicked soul.)

In a propaganda stunt, Amr Adeeb stands on a tank to praise the military coup for its great service to the security of Egypt.

In a western country, a woman flashing her sexuality in such provocative manner goes unnoticed. But, in Islamic nations, muslims question the possibilities of destroying the fibers of Islamic values by using women as sex objects. Most muslim families strive to nurture their daughters to become successful professionals, mothers, wives, daughters, and grandmothers. Therefore, this photo places Adeeb in a moral conundrum as a hypocrite who would not like to see his own daughter or wife in such unsavvy appearance.

The TV host **Lamees El Hadidi**, the wife of the TV host Amr Adeeb, the two were among two secular outlets permitted to work by the military coup.

All Islamic TV channels were closed and their hosts arrested and imprisoned. Lamees elevated Mubarak to the level of a holy authority and engaged in all fabrications and lies to support the military coup.

Mohamed Morsi refused to shut down her TV channels, as he did to all other TV channels. Morsi' kindness and tolerance turned against him and led to his ousting, arrest, and imprisonment.

Amr Adeeb, a fan of western democracy and graduate from British educational institution, Adeeb combines the two odd habits of glorifying America as the heaven for democracy, civilization, and scientific ingenuity with the opposite of portraying America as the greatest Satan that cannot be trusted, that stands behind all tragedies in the world.

Adeeb questioned Senator **John McCain** about his belief that America was so fond of Muslim Brotherhood, supportive of them since the 1950's, and aiding, funding, and supporting them in Turkey, Syria, and Egypt.

It is clear that, western secular figures in Egypt lack any credibility in gaining the trust of laypeople on the streets. Even Islamists trading in religion and gaining financially by issuing fatwas in support of figures of authority are either criticized incessantly or killed by nationals.

That paved the road to the rise of Mohamed Morsi and Muslim Brothers and compelled the two to serve national interests and the Palestinian cause.

2.2. Implicating Quranic Verses in Prophetic Predictions

2.2.1. Jews in Quran

The figurative nature of Quranic canons permitted vast spectrum of people's perception of the nature of God, the human limits of the prophets, and scope of application of heavenly canons.

Far from the long ingrained mystification of Jesus and Mary in Christianity, to the extent that many Christians omit the obvious fact the personification of **Jesus or Mary** diminishes the purpose of religious conviction, some muslims confuse Quran as a written futuristic chronicles.

Sheikh **Wagdi Ghoneim** is among the believers in the mysterious powers of Quran. He was expelled and chased out of Egypt for his literal interpretation of Quran. In the United States of America, sheikh Ghoneim was interrogated by Immigration officials for claiming that Jews were described by Allah as distorters of scriptures. Ghoneim answered that was his job as an Imam to interpret the Quran and teach people that God created Jews in such deformed manner.

Sheikh Ghoneim, who has many great and brilliant interpretations of the Quranic verses, also makes the opposite interpretation and swears by the God of the Black Rock. Ghoneim also has many poor habits that taint Islam with his shallow education and superstitious views.

Hosni Mubarak was among those brutal and ignorant military officers who devastated Egypt with poverty, corruption, and anarchy and who chased Wagdi Ghoneim out of Egypt. Yet, Mubarak's fall was in no way fair punishment for a man who ruined the future of 90 million Egyptians over thirty years. It shows that Ghoneim's beliefs in heavenly canons did too little to advance the ordained canons of God compared to armed Jihad.

Ghoneim goes farther to claim that a single Dirham (unit of money in some countries) in **usury** is equal to thirty six acts of adultery in God's ordained canons. Such mystification of Quranic verses is one among many reasons that strengthened the secular oppositions to Islamic leaders, accusing them as having obsolete and detached minds unfit to rule.

Even though all muslims waging verbal wars against Jews for their racial cleansing of Palestine and their crazy beliefs that Jews are chosen people of God, those same muslims are damaged, expelled or imprisoned or hung by muslim despots, not by Jewish invaders.

While imprisoned after his removal, Hosni Mubarak told a story about his meeting with Benjamin Netanyahu. (Published by the Youm7.com) Mubarak asked Netanyahu about his knee which was bothering him. That friendly atmosphere encouraged Netanyahu to get a map, place it in front of Mubarak, and ask Mubarak if he could help move the Palestinians out of Gaza Strip to Sinai by giving them a piece of land in Sinai. Mubarak responded: "Do you want us to go to war again?"

In the same manner that Zionist Jews dreamed by erecting a pure Jewish state between Euphrates and Nile rivers, Orthodox Muslims believe that Islam should be spread among mankind with Jihad. That entails many levels, starting by oath or Shahada and ending by the sword.

The difference between the **Islamic expansionism** and Jewish expansionism is that the former aim at spreading **Sharia Law** of heavenly canons, the latter aim at expelling non-Jews from their homes, replacing them by Jews.

If Jews were ruled by muslim Arabs, they would have faced the same massacres of Rabaa Al-Adawiya, Nahda, Presidential Palace, or Libyan, Syrian, or Iraqi destructions. As most Jewish merchants in the ancient Arabic communities were known for being **well-trusted traders**, our muslim rulers embarrassed Islam by our tyrannical regimes.

The Arab Spring was such surgical necessity to eradicate the cancer of corrupt muslim rulers.

2.2.2. Democracy in Quran

The Islamic faction of Salafi muslims could be easily accused by such charges of viewing Quran as a futuristic chronicles. Ironically, most of the Salafi's predictions, stances, and holdings proved more realistic than those based on objective analysis.

The latest among those was a Salafi's holding that **"democracy is a sort of Kufer"** or rejection of heavenly canons. Such holding preceded the ousting of Mohamed Morsi, who was elected through fair democratic process yet removed by his minister of defense. El-Sissi lacks any legal bases for interrupting the first democratic process in the history of Egypt.

Morsi restrained himself from all aggressive actions against civilian protesters, allowed all TV stations and newspapers to work without state interference, and managed the violence in Sinai with the least causalities.

In contrast, the coup leader El-Sissi, who accused Morsi for terrorizing innocent people, El-Sissi killed thousands of unarmed civilians, imprisoned many thousands of islamists, blocked all Islamic TV stations, and announced state emergency allover Egypt.

Salafi's suspicious views towards the secular makeup of Egypt were in fact more realistic than that held by Muslim Brotherhood.

The Salafi's rejection of democracy is rooted in the meaning of "salafi" or the **believers of founding fathers**. Islamic salafis or founding fathers were not elected. They came to power after proven records of assisting Prophet Muhammad triumph on Kouraish. Their indisputable faith alone led to the spread of Islam. All rulers rose to power through democratic elections appealed to the mood of the masses, not to their yearning to heavenly justice. Justice is all that Egypt needs.

2.2.3. Jihad in Quran

Among many of the salafis exiled to Afghanistan, Sudan, and Yemen many suffered the long and brutal torture and harassment of the Egyptian security apparatus. **Ayman Zawahiri** is among those held the extreme stance that Quran is the definitive futuristic chronicle for mankind. Despite the immediate disdain attached to Zawahiri's many terrorist actions that cost the lives of many innocent people, some Salafis consider Zawahiri the greatest Jihadist since **Salahdin**. His ability to attack America in its military and economic centers impressed many of his fans.

Zawahiri fought despite being chased by all state police and security apparatuses for many decades.

One cannot dismiss the courage of many salafis in stating the obvious when others are gripped by fear from getting imprisoned and constantly harassed by state security apparatuses. In fact, almost all Egyptian media, islamists or secular, official or opposition, adhere strictly to Zawahiri's views that America was the great Satan and that without defeating America, Islam cannot prosper.

For example, **Ibrahim Issa**, the Coptic Christian TV host and the most hateful opponents of Islam and islamists, does not spare time in accusing America in manipulating all aspects of life in Egypt. For Ibrahim Issa, whatever gets him to implicate islamists in sedition or treason, Issa wastes no time in fabricating tales against Muslim Brothers.

Ibrahim Issa knows well that the two golden words "**Israel**" and "**America**" must be used to taint Muslim Brothers for treason. Issa mastered the western marketing propaganda by incessantly repeating, in his TV broadcast, the combination of "Muslim Brothers", "Israel", "America", mixed by treason and traitors.

But, the grand master of Jihad, Ayman Zawahiri, is no Copt, masters Quranic verses and Hadeeth in his bones. Zawahiri is modestly dressed and physical fitter than Issa's swollen face and body. Zawahiri's gravitas crosses boundaries of nations despite his very scares broadcasts. The war between Coptic billionaire **Najib Sawiris** and his foot-soldier Ibrahim Issa against Ayman Zawahiri and his clandestine Al-Qaeda soldiers is a balance between **money** and **blood**. Sawiris's billions cannot buy a Salafi outspoken with silver tongue that could appeal to a billion muslims. Nor could Zawahiri's stern defense for heavenly justice unite all objective people to engage in bloody jihad.

Ayman Al-Zawahiri would have been the **Thomas Jefferson** of Egypt had not been severely oppressed and obsessed by the Egyptian secular government. **Mohamed Al-Zawahiri**, the brother of Ayman, was not less intellectual and shrewd than Ayman.

Al-Zawahiri brought attention after his role in the **9/11** attack on the USA, became the most wanted criminal after Ben Laden. Aside from the grim consequences of the destruction caused by Al-Qaeda, Al-Zawahiri is revered by many Salafi muslims as the only courageous muslim who could implement the military combat and killing by American military to deal with American's nosy intermingling with Muslim's desires to resurrect the **Caliphate state**.

Zawahiri's antagonism to non-muslim secular philosophies is not based on racial bias, because Zawahiri sanctions, plots, and executes combat killing of muslims who stand against **Sharia law**.

Thus, Zawahiri's end game has no ceiling in sight. Nothing would please Zawahiri less than eradicating **injustice and evil** from existence, regardless of how such evil could be defined and identified without unjustly hurting innocent people. The greatest determination and clarity of the two Zawahiri brothers Ayman and Mohamed only turned onto persistent agony to the tyrants, no peace to the oppressed.

After being pardoned by Mohamed Morsi and allowed to return to Egypt, **Mohamed Zawahiri** described Mohamed Morsi as an incomplete muslim and an advocate of statehood, not of the universality of Islam. Mohamed Al-Zawahiri views Islam as the universal law of heavenly justice and that statehood splits people, creates rotten corruption which leads to the end of mankind.

Again, the extreme line of thoughts adopted by **Ben Laden** and **Zawahiri** of armed Jihad as a mandate from God to uphold Islamic laws proved inevitable despite their bitter taste and bloody outcome.

Not too long after the 2001's attack on the USA by Al-Qaeda and the invasion of Afghanistan and Iraq by the America troops, the Arab Spring erupted from Tunisia to Yemen.

In Syria alone, over hundred thousands civilians were killed between 2011 and 2013, while the west refrained even from describing Basher Asad as a war criminal. The amazing and unexpected uprising of Syrian people after forty years of oppression by **Hafez Assad** and his son was only possible by the aid of islamists.

After Mubarak was thrown in prison, it was hoped that Egypt could avoid the bloody path of Syria. **El-Sissi's coup**, once again proved that Zawahiri's doctrine was true and viable, that only armed Jihad could advance Islamic justice.

With Syria entirely destroyed by its own secular government, El-Sissi in Egypt cannot grasp the power of Islam in deciding the future of Egypt. Unaware of the economic equation, El-Sissi flied helicopters with banners to praise the military achievements, parked tanks and armored vehicles in every state in main squares, and suspended the major train transportation in Egypt.

Hijacking democracy, disbanding the House of People, and kidnapping and imprisoning the elected Egyptian president Mohamed Morsi, El-Sissi is held accountable to no one, squanders the treasures of the nation according to his own desires. He claimed to fight terrorism in Egypt, when most those resorting to terror have no alternative to employment, education, or even to free living without the harassment of the Egyptian security apparatus.

Egypt has been bankrupt since 1967, when this author went to high school, in Alexandria, Egypt. By 1974, Sadat ended the state mandate to employ engineers, doctors, and teachers, thus leaving hundreds of thousands unemployed college graduates every year.

During the curfew, civilians wait until dark before they could get on the streets and fight the army. During day hours, snipers over roof tops have killed and injured thousands of rioters.

Streets are blocked by barbed wires and tanks to prevent civilian from gaining access to Tahrir Square. Only, El-Sissi supporters are allowed to go through the street blockade.

All access routes to Tahrir Square, Cairo, are blocked by the army. But, Egyptians have already invented the wheels of death by flooding the streets in millions and for many months, until tyrants fall.

Near Cairo Airport, the army exercises it heaviest presence.

This sniper is not shooting tear-gas canisters and need not even shoot to kill or use his gun at all. His bullet will explode in the brains, chests, or guts of civilian Egyptians. To understand such inexplicable desire to **kill for no gain**, the reader must live, feel, and understand what this sniper goes through.

From **womb to tomb**, those army conscripts have no education, no employment, no bed or seat in their homes beside dirty carpets on bare soil. I (the author) have delivered babies on bare soil for Egyptian peasants rearing over ten kids beside the new birth. No single member in those families could afford purchasing shoes, underwear, utensils, sewer, electricity, or clean water.

This sniper views civilians, dressed in pants and shirts or clean dresses his immortal enemies. He is deprived from what they have. His only source of liveliness is his military status. Purposeless killings will bring justice to his underworld of oppression and deprivation. He will create orphaned children and windows to equally share his sufferings.

Clearly, this sniper's life is not threatened and his **facial expressions of joy** do not show any grave danger. Those shot and injured are left handicap all life-long without any compensation, in country where large families depend on a single bread-earner to support many hungry members of the family. In many families, the sole bread earner supports his parents beside his own immediate family.

2.2.4. Secularism and Quran

One might assume that the figurative verses of Quran have created greater abilities to extrapolate and expect potential dangers, those not versed in Quran could not anticipate.

In Egypt, El-Sissi's men organized rallies lifting Gamal Abdul Nasser's posters (left) in order to portray El-Sissi as the new savior. Nasser's legacy was banned in Egypt during the forty years of Sadat and Mubarak's regimes. But, Al-Jazeera did not give El-Sissi a chance. Many heavy-weight commentators exposed the severe deficits of El-Sissi compared to Nasser's unprecedented historic impact.

In Yemen (right), the memories of Nasser's support in 1964's revolution made Yemen's pulse in synchrony with Egypt's pulse. **"God takes away from he wishes"**, the sign reads.

Without Quran, the two men Ben Laden and Ayman Zawahiri could have not succeeded in dragging the USA to Afghanistan and Iraq. That sparked the chaos in the Middle East, leading to the removal of Saddam, followed by **Ben Ali, Muammar Qaddafi, Abdullah Saleh,** and **Hosni Mubarak,** with greater pressure on the Saudi Arabia to administer true Islamic justice.

Because of the influence of Quran, El-Sissi's reverse revolution permitted only those TV stations which support his aggressive and frightening militarization of Egypt. All Quran-based TV stations were banned, their hosts imprisoned, in an era most Egyptians have access to outside TV stations and have long ingrained mistrust to the pro-government media. Among those ridiculous campaigns to polish El-Sissi's image, was the concerted plot of broadcasting Gamal Abdul **Nasser's achievements.** Thus, secularists omitted the historic memory of Quranic verses embedded in every muslim in Egypt, reverted on Nasser's legacy to lift their own hero. It should be noted that Sadat banned all speeches or broadcasting referring to Nasser's era.

Among those permitted to broadcast by El-Sissi, **Amr Adeeb** claims that the greatness of Egyptians is their achievements in 1973's crossing the Suez Canal and 2013's removal of Morsi. Adeeb attributes those greatest achievements to the Egyptian military, now headed by El-Sissi. Adeeb dismissed the forty years of suffering from 1973 and 2013 caused by the complacent military officers aided Mubarak to plunder Egypt for three decades.

In fact, the Egyptian military suffers the consequences of choosing its officers from the pool of lowest academic achievers in the nation. During the wars of 1964, 1967, and 1973, most military officers were the lowest academic achievers, trained in haste, thrown in the battle fields within months from their start in military academies. Thus, without exception, modern Egyptian military officers lack the **Quranic vocalization** and the **Quranic eloquence**; hence invoke resentment in the ears and hearts of laypeople in homes and streets.

General **Ahmed Shafik** might have won the popular vote against Mohamed Morsi and might have been cheated by his fellow military generals from being the president of Egypt.

Even though, to date Shafik hangs to those claims, he was fortunate to be kept away from his own destruction by his shallow military training, bankrupt intellect, and total lack of knowledge of Quran.

Both Generals **Mohamed Hussein Tantawi** and **Sami Hafez Anan** heeded the advice of Muhammad Hassanien Heikal to hand the presidency to Muslim Brotherhood. This has grass roots that could calm down the villages and streets of Egypt after the anarchy that followed the fall of Mubarak.

The term **"Photoshop"** entered Egypt's politics as Al-Ahram official government newspaper doctored the original photo to make Mubarak lead Obama in a meeting.

Youssef Al-Housseiny (left) and **Bassem Youssef** (right) are among those secular TV broadcasters allowed to broadcast by El-Sissi. The two did more damage to liberalism than all liberal Egyptians wish.

Youssef Al-Housseiny a self-declared communist lacks any depth or passion to Islam, favor fabrications against Muslim Brothers to appease Najib Sawiris, his Coptic employer.

Bassem Youssef, an Egyptian heart surgeon raised and bred on western values, dedicated his comical program to replicate Jon Stewart's American show. Bassem made Mohamed Morsi and Islamists his own obsession until the ousting of Morsi by the military coup. As the military coup started the bloody course, locked up all Islamists, Bassem Youssef never criticized the brutality of the coup or the delinquency of its officers.

To Bassem's misfortune, Jon Stewart's show ended like many shows that cannot make revenues. Bassem Youssef's show, despite not making revenues, still lives on foreign funding by Sawiris and other billionaires dreading Islam and Muslim Brothers.

Turkey reversed the secular liberal trend in 2000's and was able to triple the **average annual income** of its people in ten years. Turkey proved to the European Union, which rejected its participation in it, that Turkey could restore its Islamic glory anew on its own terms.

One cannot deny the historic trends that military forces have always succeeded oppressing generations of free minds in the communist bloc and most muslim nations. From 1945 till 1991, the Communist bloc survived 45 years, imprisoned many millions of Europeans behind iron gate. Similar oppressions of the same average duration took place in Egypt, Syria, and Yemen. Saudi Arabia was unique in imprisoning its population behind the most oppressive authoritarian regime for eighty years.

The burden of political oppression reflected clearly on the public health. The four wealthiest Arab nations **Saudi Arabia, Kuwait, Bahrain,** and **Qatar** rank on top of nations where diabetes prevalence exceeds 14%. In contrast, **Russian Federation** and the **United States of America** fall under the 12% prevalence of diabetes.

International Diabetes Federation. Diabetes Atlas 5th Edition - Country Estimates Table 2011

Rank	Diabetes national prevalence (%)	Country/territory
7	16.21	Saudi Arabia
8	15.94	Kuwait
13	15.29	Bahrain
15	15.16	Egypt
23	14.07	Qatar
35	11.54	Russian Federation
42	10.94	United States of America

In particular, **Diabetes mellitus** is best indicator for the quality of life of proper nutrition and physical activity. Ironically, the four nations where Islam was first born and thrived ended on the top of nations inflicted by ignorance in nutrition, physical education, and democratic practices.

Not because those medical sciences were distinctly different from Islamic sciences, since Islam elevates persons of knowledge above those who lack knowledge, but also because those Islamic nations adopted the most rejected values in Islam such as **entitlement by birth** of kings and royal members, monopolizing the treasures of their nations in their own personal favors.

In such bleak Islamic reversal by the Islam's own guardians rose Osama Ben Laden seeking resurrection of Islam into its initial core values of equality and justice based on deeds, not on blood ties.

Instead of working within the Saudi system bring change, Ben Laden realized the impossibility to turn the tide of ignorance, complacency, cronyism, and nepotism within the Bedouin tribes of Arabia. Ben Laden dreamt of building an Islamic nation from scratch on the liberated Afghanistan territories.

As the linguistic and cultural challenges interfered between Ben Laden and his dreams, he resorted to the most desperate plots of reeking havoc amongst his perceived enemies and the friends of his enemy, the United States and Israel. Even though **Ben Laden** and **Zawahiri** suffered enormously on the hands of their own native people, both men never appreciated the Jewish struggle to build own nation. **Israel can defend Jews against the oppression of Saudi Arabia and Egypt**, while the Saudis and Egyptians must die to defend themselves from their own despots.

True that Jews cleansed Palestine from its native owners, the Palestinians, yet Bashar Asad broke the Zionist record by expelling more than five million Syrians from their homes and murdering over hundred thousands by weapons of military warfare.

Ben Laden fought the same enemies which Zionist Jews fought, with the exception that Jews organized a viable nation that could be defended against Arab despots. Ben Laden engaged in short sighted terror attacks that only annoyed his enemies, never achieved higher purposes.

2.2.5. Shia and Quran

One must also consider the two mortal enemies of salafis Ben Laden and Ayman Zawahiri, namely; **Shia muslims** and **Zionist Jews**, when considering the mystification of Quran and its implicating in futuristic chronicles of mankind.

The **Shia's mystification** of Quran and their ability to centralize military power in the hands of Imams is attributed to the mastery of deception of illiterate population in the battle for survival against Sunnis' aggression. Shia mystification of Quran runs against the advances in society and exposes the rots of fabrication and deception.

Shias conferred heavenly power on Imams, deprived the majority of their followers from the individual choices of criticism and inquisition. The result was the ability of Iran to stand steadfast against Saddam, but fell in the trap of sectarian violence and discrimination in Syria.
In Syria, the bulk of Sunni populations sensed the menace of Shia aggression and was compelled to weigh the danger between **Zionist aggression** and **Shia's aggression.**

The arrival of Mohamed Morsi to power and the concerted effort of Saudis to sabotage Morsi's stampede to establishing greater Islamic power, Morsi lent on the Shias of Iran for help. That immediately invoked the Salafis' anger and led to immediate execution of **Sheikh Hassan Shihata**, in Giza, Egypt in 2013.

The murder of Shihata exposed many previously unknown obsessions of Shia's teachings. Even though Egyptians are exposed to the Coptic condescending propaganda against Prophet Muhammad, they understood that the followers of the cross are expected to hate Muhammad.

An Egyptian Copt **Nakoula Basseley** fabricated stories about Prophet Muhammad in an American made movie "**Innocence Of muslims**". Muslims view the Coptic resentment of Muhammad as a natural course of the adoption of Christianity in lieu of Islam. That is not the case when it comes to Shia muslims launching incessant insults against the associates of Muhammad, as was the case with Hassan Shihata.

Iranian Shia incurred over two millions killed for the sake of defending the Islamic Revolution from Saddam's aggression, funded and supported by Saudis, Kuwaitis, America, and Israel.

Their rivals, the Salafis, faced the same fate in Tunisia, Libya, Yemen, Syria and Egypt. This time, the blood shed is the long awaited and anticipated battle against the real Arab despots.

In Sudan, the historically implanted Christianity in the south finally succeeded in receding the south from the north, resulting into two impoverished and bankrupt nations.

In Sinai, the Salafis and Muslim Brotherhoods must get along with their morbid enemy, Shia muslims, in order to arm Hamas in Gaza strip to ward off Israeli aggression. In addition, they must fight the Egyptian army which empowered Hosni Mubarak to plunder Egypt for thirty years.

Turning Sinai into another Afghanistan might be the strongest card which Islamists could use in changing the map of the Middle East.

Inside Egypt, Salafis and Muslim Brothers control the streets and could easily drain the energy of the foolish military planning to implement emergency laws, after the failure of those laws to avert the ousting of Mubarak.

The Coptic nail in the back of Salafis, and the well-established cowardice of Coptic authorities in supporting despots and military rulers, led to the burning of 52 churches within days after the massacre of Rabaa Adawiya.

But, the Egypt's inner anarchy will undoubtedly lead to loss on all sides, muslims, Copts, or Jews. Here, there are 90 million people with plenty of animosity against the government oppressors and plenty of resources to administer justice under the power of guns, without the need for the morbidly corrupt Egyptian judicial system.

It suffices to say that Egyptian courts have notorious history of protracting litigation over decades and making politically motivated verdicts.

Ahmad Badreddin Hassoun, the mofti of Syria (sitting), and Bashar Assad (standing).

Hassooun is no better than Ahmed Tayyib (current mofti of Egypt) or **Ali Goumaa,** the notorious fabricator and ex-mofti of Egypt. Hassooun supported Assad in the two year destruction of Syria. Assad was the first president in history to use the army and air force to destroy his own nation and kill his citizens. Bashar Assad succeeded in getting Russia to supply him with lethal weapons that can be used to destroy his people.

As the Egyptian secretary of Mubarak, Mustafa El-Fiqi explains, the United States will not attack Syria or remove Assad as long as Assad keeps fighting and killing. The USA did the same in Iraq. That would weaken Syria and eliminate its danger on Israel.

El-Fiqi explains that Israel is the **entry access** to the White House. In an incident of a Tunisian official in need for financial support from the United State, he was told to follow the procedure that takes many months to achieve his goal. The Tunisian official telephoned Benjamin Netanyahu while on trip to Russia, asked him to intervene on his behalf in the White House in change for giving Netanyahu a chance to talk to a muslim crowd before returning to Israel. Netanyahu accepted the deal. The Tunisian official was sitting in the White House within days.

Ahmad Badreddin Hassoun, a Shia Muslim Imam thrives on the tyranny of Assad. This led to the second wave of wars between Sunnis and Shias, after the Iraqi's conflict.

As the American plot was exposed in the handling of power in Iraq to Shias, the entire Gulf states felt the conspiracy between Shias and Americans aimed at maintain continuing wars in the Middle East.

Egyptian Shia **Imam Hassan Shihata** was murdered in a house in Giza of Egypt by angry Sunni muslims during the onslaught on the Sunnis by Hezballah in Syria.

Shihata has a long history with the Egyptian security police after his own son reported his father's maniacal attacks on the associates of prophet Muhammad. Apparently, Shihata was inflicted by mental illness not religious bigotry, because his insults to the associates of Prophet Muhammad were purely theatrical, obscene, and epithetical, not serving any purpose of teaching or strengthening faith.

Egyptian Shia **Imam Hassan Shihata** body was dragged by rioters after his repeated beating to death. Shihata visited a house in Giza to preach Shia's Islamic teaching, where people warned him form going there. His attackers used heavy hammers to penetrate the ceiling of the house, even though they could have burnt it, captured Hassan Shihata, and rejoiced his beating to death.

Few weeks later, after the ousting of Mohamed Morsi and the massacre of Rabaa Al-Adawiya, the providence of **Giza** was the scenes of massacring the police sheriff and his staff followed by shooting the head of police who came to capture the killers.

Outside Egypt, this young Shia sheikh **Yasser Al-Habib** did not bother to review the maddening insults made by Imam Hassan Shihata on YouTube videos. Habib considered Shihata a martyr of Islam and his killers are "Kafereen" and that Hassan Shihata was a giant illuminator. Yasser Al-Habib, like Muqtada El-Sadr thrives on the fanatic trade in religion to control illiterate followers.

After 40 years of Hafez Assad's iron grip on the Syrian people, people's anger finally exceeded the threshold of public complacency. Armed resistance, burning, bombing, and killing became the sole mean of change in Syria.

2.2.6. Puritanical Salafis and Quran

Regardless of the imperfection of the views of muslim Salafis on the future of an Islamic society and the grave obstacle of having millions of Copts bred and nurtured to adopt the magic and superstition of the Orthodox Christian churches, Salafis confront even greater obstacle of extreme **Jewish apartheid** in Palestine.

In Sinai, international mandates allow Israelis to enter Sinai without visas and prohibit Egyptians from interfering with the violation of Israelis of the civil rights of Palestinians. Those mandates were born out of **Henry Kissinger**'s doctrine of dealing with Arab nations as countries lacking their Arabic and Islamic heritages.

Those two problems however have been imposed on the realities of the Middle East for seven decades or more. Their present revival is attributed mainly to the **unbearable economic situations** which behoove all Egyptians to seek the real roots of corruption in the Egyptian government and military.

As the Salafis breathed relief with the ousting of Mohamed Morsi and the perspectives of having more conservative Islamic system, Salafis confronted the gravest reality that the previous security apparatus of Mubarak and Mubarak's men have returned to their previous positions, all muslim activists were locked up, all Islamic media outlets closed, and national emergency law returned the way it was for thirty years.

The puritanical views of salafism are best advocated by **Safwat Hegazy.** He is among the most charismatic and eloquent Salafis, helped bring down Mubarak, elect Morsi, fought El-Sissi, and supported Muslim Brothers despite his rejection to the principal of centralized control of "Murshid" or Islamic Guidance.

Hegazy mixed vividly between superstitious power of faith and realistic political powers. He stressed on the rejection of islamists and the new generations to any leader who put military badges on his shoulders and to any members of the National Party which supported Sadat and Mubarak.

Hegazy relied heavily on the true meaning of Quran and Islam to captivate the souls of millions of muslims and spread the terror and fear in the hearts of the leaders of the military coup. Hegazy's infamous statement that inflamed the military was:

"Morsi is a red-line. Those who touch Morsi, we will spray them by blood."

Safwat Hegazy took sanctuary in Rabaa Al-Adawiya, with his young kids and wife. His daughter stood here, in front of the crowd of Rabaa Al-Adawiya, and told the world that the police was surrounding their home looking for her dad.

Hegazy was arrested while escaping to Libya, as the government news announced. Hegazy will remain in the conscience of Muslims as the voice of justice and faith, a man with great courage and charisma in times of great crises.

Military police escorting Mustafa Hegazy to prison during his arrest. Most young soldiers take photographs with those national figures of Islam for personal reasons. A secret cell phone captured a video for him, published on youtube.com, blinded and handcuffed while a soldier cursing his mother and describing him as sexual pervert. Another soldier concerned for the safety of Hegazy shouted on the crowd to be careful not to hurt him during their violent pushing and dragging him to a dark cage.

Despite the brutality and impropriety involved in torturing and silencing this man, he was well-known for forgiveness and magnanimity in mannerism. Hegazy might felt mercy for the soldier who cursed him because the soldier's voice indicated his extreme emptiness of soul and intellect. Safwat Hegazy's comments resonated in the Salafi medium, bringing forwards **Tareq Al-Zumer**, another Salafi icon, top Jihadist, and a main participant in the assassination of Sadat. Al-Zumer stated: **"On June 30, we will crush them"**.

He meant the islamists will crush the opponents of Morsi.

Tareq Al-Zumer and his uncle **Abboud Al-Zumer** are among few Islamists who changed the history of Egypt by armed Jihad, eliminated Anwar Sadat from ruling Egypt. Tareq studied law in prison. Mubarak rejected his release from military prison after the end of his 25-year sentence. Both Zumer were released with Mohamed Morsi, in the peak of anarchy of the January 25 revolution. Mustafa Al-Fiqi accused Gamal Mubarak for opening the prisons in order to spread chaos, then return as a savior.

Tareq Al-Zumer exploited the 30-year in prison in polishing his legal shrewdness and appeared as the new Savior of the Islamic Project. He was arrested and sent back to prison by El-Sissi with newly fabricated charges.

Even though both Hegazy and Zumer predicted the future precisely, as both were the most intellectual and the shrewdest Islamic minds in Egypt in their own times, both were caught and imprisoned, while the Egyptian streets engulfed in blood bathes.

That was not the first time in history that Tareq Al-Zumer told the Egyptians: "**I told you so**". In 1981, he plotted the removal of Sadat, which vindicated the Egyptians from the fatal errors made by Sadat in compromising the Palestinian cause and spreading corruption in Egypt.

As for Hegazy, the man combined serious flaws of fictional thinking and the greatest eloquence in rendering the Quranic canons living souls. Regardless of Hegazy's imperfection, one cannot deny the man's exceptional support for the principal of democratically elected president and his crystal clear prediction that the removal of the president by military coup will leave no chance to have any democratically elected president.

Hegazy made it clear that:

"If they take out Morsi and bring a new president, we will go the presidential palace and bring their man down as we did with Mubarak."
Yet, Hegazy went farther to claim:
"If we want to make it all-Islamic nation, what prevents us from doing so?"

Safwat Hegazy, though enjoying the most transparent Islamic mind of his generation, did not grasp the great danger of **military and police forces** established from the illiterate and lowest academic performers in society. Most Egyptians harbor contempt to the rigid and difficult military life-style geared to worship the top corrupt general and crush all lower ranks. In addition, the Egyptian military excludes islamists from military services and marginalizes Copts to the extreme.

Hence, Safwat Hegazy's idealistic and academic prediction that the Islamic Caliphate has just begun by Morsi was interrupted, if not reversed, by the bloody coup of El-Sissi and the slipping of Egypt into total bloody chaos.

2.2.7. Compromise in Quran

As puritanical Salafis have their means of turning Quran onto the crystal ball of the future, they got all the ingredients that could carve a scenario from the remote past that mimics the irrational and reckless strategies of the June 30, 2013's military coup of Egypt.

Mohamed Morsi was removed arrested, and imprisoned without charges by his subordinate Abdul Fattah El-Sissi. Morsi was democratically elected. In contrast, Hosni Mubarak was allowed to rule until many people were killed when it became impossible to keep millions in the streets under control for any length of time. Mubarak was not arrested or detained many months after his ousting by the people.

Prior to ousting Morsi, **El-Sissi** threatened Morsi on June 26, 2013 to take unprecedented actions if Morsi does not compromise. That was both illegal and illogical for a democratically elected president to be threatened by his subordinate.

Meanwhile, El-Sissi encouraged protesters to pour onto the streets, long before June 30, and participated passively and aggressively in creating the state of anarchy that gives him the excuse to conduct a military coup. El-Sissi conveyed to world the false news that **thirty million** Egyptians marched on the streets against Morsi.

El-Sissi's claim was false because it amounted to revolt by 1 in 3 Egyptians, including children, women, elderly, rural, and urban inhabitants. It is even impossible to prove that ten million people could be documented, photographed, or located in such vast geography of Egypt where 90 million people are spread along the River Nile and its Delta.

El-Sissi's lies kept pouring every passing day after his coup.

Before the coup, when 40 or so were killed in Suez Canal and port Sayyid, Mohamed Morsi was severely rebuked by both domestic and foreign sources for enacting for a month **emergency state** in those cities. After the coup, El-Sissi enacted emergency law allover Egypt for one year, suspended all train transportations, and sent military tanks, helicopters, and troops to many cities to contain violence.

The **unprecedented massacres** in front of the presidential palace, in Rabaa Adawiya, Nahda square, and many wide-spread massacres that followed, all carved the bloody agenda of the old school military coup.

El-Sissi's alleged plan, to **restore rapport** between the president, the judicial system, the deep-state remains of Mubarak, the military, and street protesters, turned into a targeted plan to arrest and annihilate the Muslim Brotherhood, pan their participation in politics, arrest and detain all associated with Muslim Brotherhood, and capture and freeze all assets owned by Muslim Brotherhood.

Somehow, El-Sissi never learned the lessons of the contemporary history that oppression led to bloody confrontation.

Also, somehow, El-Sissi discounted the extreme financial difficulty that faced Egypt since January 25, 2011 to date and the inevitable need to protect democracy rather than initiate anarchy.

In similar military coup in Russia, **Boris Yeltsin** stood on a tank to defy the military coup on August 18, 1991, against **Gorbachev**. But El-Sissi was too blind to see the bloody future of Egypt where criminal military and police generals hijacked democracy, killed thousands of civilians, plundered Egypt to the Dark Ages.

El-Sissi bought into **Muhammad Hassaenien Heikal**'s tale on **Charles de Gaulle's** example to justify that Mohamed Morsi should have resigned. Heikal knew well the plot of trapping and sabotaging the islamic project in order to create chaos and reverse the democratic process dreamed of by millions of hopeless Egyptians.

In every Egyptian home, democracy amounted to winning over the other side by a single vote. Whoever wins leads both supporters and adversaries to the end of the term.

Morsi received 13,230,131 votes (51.73%), **Ahmed Shafik**, 12,347,380 (48.27%). After the military coup, the thirteen million votes for Morsi were wiped out by a single Army officer, El-Sissi.

El-Sissi took the Oath in front of Morsi. El-Sissi was able to resign to pose his disagreement with Morsi.

Comically, El-Sissi ousted Morsi, appointed **Adly Mansour** the new temporary president, then took the new Oath in front of the Adly Mansour, whom he has just appointed.

That infuriated Recep Tayyib Erdoğan, the Prime Minister of Turkey. Erdoğan rebuked **Mohamed ElBaradie** for taking the Oath in front of Adly Mansour. The latter appointed by El-Sissi. ElBaradie failed to get elected to any position and arrived to power on the back of military tanks. ElBaradie seems to have grasped that rebuke very well, bailed out of El-Sissi's comical military coup as soon as Rabaa Adawiya massacre was committed.

El-Sissi has then to overcome the internal and external unease over his mandate to hijack democracy, solely, based on his personal judgment and on his unprecedented request to Egyptians to get out on the streets to give him authorization to **fight terrorism**. As if the 90 million Egyptians were too dumb to reject El-Sissi's illogical excuses. For, the military has no training or mandate to define, find, or fight terrorism.

ElBaradie was famous for criticizing Morsi for adopting security solution for political failures. Now, El-Sissi lacks any political solutions, depends entirely on containing street riots, totally oblivious to the growing economic crises.

Outside, El-Sissi got Obama to accept the idea that popular election is no substitute for presidential competence in running the nation. Sure, Obama would have never accepted a military coup in America against **George W. Bush**, when Bush's popularity plummeted to 25% in 2008. Nor would any western citizen sanction the idea of military officers taking over civilian lives or breaking the law.

Recep Tayyib Erdoğan, the Prime Minister of Turkey, was instrumental in getting **Mohamed ElBaradie** to get grip with reality, which led to his resignation from El-Sissi's coup government. Erdoğan wept on hearing the news of the death of **Asma Beltagy**.

General **Ahmed Shafik**, who lost election in front of Morsi, flocked Egypt after being indicted for embezzlement. In his exile in Qatar, Shafik described the Muslim Brothers unfit to run Egypt because they were prisoners for sixty years and that he had better CV than islamists, whom he described as being able only to run a grocery store.

Not only that Shafik was close to Mubarak and appointed by him to run the new government during the riots of January 25, 2012, but that Shafik's **military background** created wide resentment against any figure from the agency that plundered Egypt for sixty years. Further, Shafik's claim that the injustice inflicted on islamists during the previous three administrations disqualified the oppressed from governing Egypt and placed him as a better qualified candidate, shows the serious detachment of Shafik from basic Quranic canons.

The jailer Shafik claims to be better qualified because he was free while those jailed by his tyrannical regime lack his experience as an oppressor and tyrant for sixty years.

Mustafa Bakry (left) and Tawfeek Okasha (right) are among those opportunists enriched themselves through Mubarak' corruption.

Bakry adopted the tactic of personal destruction in favor to billionaires interested in spreading chaos in Egypt.

Okasha is a typical rural swindler, thrived through Mubarak's era, and succeeded in retrieving the properties lost when Nasser restricted ownership of farming land on the wealthy.

Okasha comprises an icon of hypocrisy, comedy, and fabrication on the Egyptian landscape. Okasha's delusion let him run for the presidency of Egypt, when many ridiculed his lack of insight into his true status in society. He was chased by a woman he married for an hour and admitted on open public TV that he married the woman at 12:00 noon, divorced her at 1:30 PM on the same day.

The woman has a child with official records that Okasha was his father. On regular occasions, Okasha received warning notices that he would be arrested by court orders in cases filed against him by his ex-wife. In all arrest orders, the arresting police officers are bribed by Okasha in order to let him sneak out of the TV building, until the police announces that Okasha evaded capture.

Amidst the atmosphere of anarchy and reverse revolution, the journalist **Mustafa Bakry**, well-known snitch and opportunist, supported figures of power and profited from his mastery of snitching, came to the help of Ahmed Shafik.

Initially, Shafik was accused for bribery in purchasing airplanes from Boeing during Mubarak's era. The Muslim Brothers figured out Shafik's unexplained enrichment and the exaggerated pricing of the airplanes. Yet after Morsi was ousted, Bakry claimed that the airplanes were more expensive when first produced in 2005 and their current lower prices were due to the higher demand on them.

It was the same Bakry who waited until Mubarak was ousted to file criminal charges against Suzanne Mubarak and her sons for money laundering, Bakry has no evidence to support his claims as he did in implicating Mubarak, only after his ousting.

In an article entitled "**Fighting Bribery out of Self-Interest**", by **Frederik Richter**, Mustafa Bakry the editor in chief of the independent weekly newspaper "Al Osbou" or "The Week", published a series of articles about Ibrahim Nafie. The latter was until July of that year the head of the state press agency **Al-Ahram**. Bakry listed in embarrassing details that Nafie had pocketed half million dollars per year, disguised as commissions for the sale of advertising. Bakry claimed that, over the course of his more than 20 years in office, Nafie has accumulated 70 million dollars. Bakry exercised the same ambush tactic against Mubarak and was rebuked on air by a retired judge for breaching private bank security rules in order to achieve personal gain.

As Bakry became known as a snitch in favor of the powerful and during his support to El-Sissi, activists rioted in front of Bakry's mansion seeking explanation for the exuberant price of a house owned by Bakry through illegal means. Bakry showed up, fired his gun in the air to scare the protesters and bragged about walking around armed as a tough man from the South.

Soon after Morsi's ousting, Shafik returned to Egypt declaring his intent to run for presidency only if the people insisted he should. Shafik latter changed his mind and stated that he would run for presidency if El-Sissi does not run.

Such hesitation was also well-known about **Amr Mousa** who kept repeating his promise to run for presidency only if Mubarak does not run. Thus, the two old dogs described by most Egyptians as relics from the past, Amr Moussa and Ahmed Shafik, could not pass basic Quranic tests on virtues or ward off injustice inflicted on millions of Egyptians.

Salafis need not invoke Quranic canons in order to reject the **fickleness** of Mousa or Shafik, since even the agents of Mubarak, like Amr Adeeb came harsh against Shafik for showing such unsettling ambiguity in his stance. Both men, Mousa and Shafik, have long learned that **big cats should not fight**.

The Egyptian people could not find better than Islamists during the grim economic situation when compromise amounts to suicide. Mohamed ElBaradie and others kept dragging **Nelson Mandela**'s example as model for forgiving and forgetting. In a culture where only connected individuals could survive, others perish, forgiving does not level the field for the deprived to survive. Also, forgetting the sins of the billionaires, when hundreds of thousands of Islamists are still kept in prisons, distresses those already crushed in poverty and despair.

2.3. Wishful Faith

2.3.1. Imposing Demands on the Divine

The very narrow, ineffective, and illogical interpretation of prayers by many muslim imams and sheikhs overloads Quranic verses with confusion, mistrust, and disdain.

Imams and sheikhs leading muslim followers, prayed to God on loud speakers, asking God to freeze the blood in the arteries of Abdul Fattah El-Sissi and to turn the dogs of El-Sissi against him.

Not too long afterwards, those demagogues were arrested and thrown in prisons by El-Sissi's attack dogs and thousands of muslim followers were shot by exploding bullets that shattered their brains, guts, and bones.

In Qatter, more than a thousand miles east to Egypt, sheikh **Wagdi Ghoneim** launches constant prayers to God seeking the victory to the oppressed Egyptians and the destruction of El-Sissi.

In front of the Presidential Palace, muslim protesters gathered at dawn to pray. Fifty two of the prayers were shot from behind and many hundreds injured by El-Sissi's attack dogs.

2.3.2. Expecting the Divine to Restore Welfare

On July 3, 2013, when the military coup ousted Mohamed Morsi, one of the top leaders of Muslim Brotherhoods; Dr. **Essam Elerian**, published the following verse from sura **Al-Isra**:

مع قران الفجر والاية (16) من سورة [الإسراء] وقوله تعالى :

" وإذا أردنا أن نهلك قرية أمرنا مترفيها ففسقوا فيها فحق عليها القول فدمرناها تدميرا." صدق الله العظيم.

تأمل سنة الله الماضية ،وقف عند الألفاظ الآتية في الآية الكريمة: أردنا ،فهو صاحب الإرادة المطلقة.وقوله أمرنا اى أمر كوني.وقوله مترفيها.وحق عليها القول. والله اعلم.

This is translated as follows:

Al-Isra (The Night Journey)

****
(16) And when We decide to destroy a town, We send a definite order (to obey Allâh and be righteous) to those among them [or We (first) increase in number those of its population] who lead a life of luxury. Then, they transgress therein, and thus the word (of torment) is justified against it (them). Then, We destroy it completely.
****

Thus, **Essam Elerian** invokes the Quran to describe the status quo in the Egyptian society and then predict that God will destroy the wicked.

However, Elerian knew well after many decades of imprisonments and oppression that the town he was elected to govern was inflected with the wickedness from which he claims that God would reverse.

Three days later, on July 6, 2013, Elerian cited the following four verses from sura Al-**Shuara (The Poets)**:

الخاطرة القرآنية من آيات سورة (الشعراء):
" وتوكّل على العزيز الرحيم، الذي يراك حين تقوم،وتقلبك
فى الساجدين.إنه هو السميع العليم." صدق الله العظيم،

1/ التوكّل هو الثقة فى الله من أخذ الأسباب وعدم الاعتماد عليها ،بل تعليق الرجاء فى الله وحده.

2/ الوصف بالعزيز بمعنى أنه لا يغلبه أحد وهو القاهر فوق عباده ،والوصف بالرحيم يدل على انه أرسله صلى الله عليه وسلم، وأساند بالرحمة الإلهية لكل العالمين بما فيهم المخالفين.

3/ إنه سبحانه يحب أن يرى عبده حال قيامه بين يديه بالليل والنهار خاشعا منيبا ومنتصرا منتذلا ليعلم أنه ترك راحته ولذته ليقف بين يدي مولاه يطلب دعمه وتأييده ورضاه.

3/ التقلب فى الساجدين هو الانتقال من حال إلى حال فى حال قيامه بتنوع صور الأعمال حسب وارات الأحوال الذى ترد على القلب فيتقلب من ضعف إلى قوة ومن ذل إلى عزة والله يريد منك أن تكون متعه وحده على أى حال وكل حال.

4/ إنه هو السميع لكل شاردة ووارده ،بسمعك وبسمع غيرك من المجرمين المعاصرين، وهو العليم بكل شئ وكل أمر فلا تحزن ولا تيأس فأنت فى نصحه وقد نهالك عن الشرك،وأمرك بالمبادرة على الدعوة خاصة الفرديس وخفض الجناح لمن اتبعك من المؤمنين.

The translation of those verses is as follows:

Al-Shuara (The Poets)
****

(217) And put your trust in the All-Mighty, the Most Merciful,
(218) Who sees you (O Muhammad) when you stand up.
(219) And your movements among those who fall prostrate (to Allâh in the five compulsory congregational prayers).
(220) Verily, He, only He, is the All-Hearer, the All-Knower.
(221) Shall I inform you (O people!) upon whom the devils descend?
****

Even though Quran depicts God as all-hearer, all-knower, the invocation of literal Quranic verses in the extreme times of difficulty, when Essam Elerian had been involved in lengthy election process and struggle to arrive to power, which his party lost to the military coup, shows the schism between the intellectual belief in Quran and invocation of Quranic figurative canons to justify failure in management and plotting.

To his credit, Dr. Essam Elerian was the only Muslim Brother who evaded capture by El-Sissi to this date, while his fellows were captured from their homes, arrested, and imprisoned.

2.3.3. Rejecting the Divine Altogether

One might argue that the Muslim Brothers, including Essam Elerian, adopted the Quranic wisdom of taking the high roads in the most dismal environment of a nation infested by corruption throughout all government branches. The Muslim Brothers arrived to presidential power by fair and legitimate election. They lost power to a coup, but with crystal clear record and reputation for being kind, peaceful, and law abiding citizens.

In contrast, El-Sissi's military coup appointed 19 military generals of 25 provincial governors' positions throughout Egypt. In Alexandria providence, the newly appointed governor, General **Tareq Mahdi Abdul Tawab Mohamed** shunned citizens complaining that they cannot find food or job. The military governor ordered the audience to shut up, accused them by being liars.

The same governor was caught on video threatening the police who do not fire on civilians to be shot.

El-Sissi held the greatest celebration of October 6th amidst state of emergency law. The celebration led to greater killings and injuries. Only 40,000 picked people showed up in the celebration, many of them were foreigners.

محافظ الإسكندرية

لواء اركان حرب / طارق مهدى عبد التواب محمد
محافظ محافظة الاسكندرية
فى 13 اغسطس, 2013

The news that General **Tareq Mahdi Abdul Tawab Mohamed** would be the new man of El-Sissi to rule Alexandria, Egypt, was another blow to the coup.

The governor of Alexandria, General **Tareq Mahdi Abdul Tawab Mohamed**, newly appointed by El-Sissi, shouts on the audience and accuses them by lying, when they claimed that they have not been paid for six months, they cannot find food or jobs.

This sign was put in the face of the governor: "**Six months without salaries. We are dying.**"

The governor of Alexandria, General **Tareq Mahdi Abdul Tawab Mohamed**, might have serious mental history that was kept unknown to the public. The General ordered audience to "shut up" in an epileptic fit, waving his arms and body, while being video taped.

In his prison, Hosni Mubarak described Muslim Brothers as "**a dog found a bone, will bite on it to death.**" Mubarak claimed that the United States started pressing him to leave power since 2005 AD. He claimed that he told the Americans that would be giving up his job on 2011.

Thus, Mubarak never sensed that holding to power for 30 years created tragic destruction of Egypt, while the 11 months of rule by Muslim Brothers was a bone in the jaws of a vicious dog.

The above logic of attempting to erect a **Utopian Islamic society** has deflected attention from the painful decades of Mubarak's oppression onto the issue of imperfection and detachments of islamists.

In fact, if islamists refrained completely from replacing Mubarak's heavy burden of corruption and widespread economic crises, Muslim Brothers could have prepared their youth to cope with the trickeries of politics and organized their grass roots to replace the dysfunctional police and security system.

The haphazard aggregation of puritanical religious herd exaggerated the detachments of islamists and clouded many viable solutions that could have succeeded in reversing the tide in their favor.

Even today, Muslim Brothers and Salafis could still win by moving to the background, staying low, unseen, and unheard. El-Sissi will show his emptiness, the exact mindset of Mubarak's most hated dullness in sensing the pulse of time and people.

As Mubarak's deep state organized concerted campaign accusing Mohamed Morsi by excluding non-islamists from the government, the military coup leader, El-Sissi appointed 19 generals to the positions of governors.

This general and the new governor of Alexandria lacked any basic skill in dealing with public, threatened soldiers by severe punishments if they refused to fire on protesters, and accused unemployed people, seeking jobs and food, for being liars.

CHAPTER 3

Al-Azhar

3.1. Al-Azhar Mission

Al-Azhar was built by **Jawhar Al-Siqilli** in 970 AD as "The mosque of Cairo". Today, Al-Azhar is a university comprised of many colleges in physical and religious sciences. Its contemporary rule comprises the formal state religious authority. The influence of the state on the directions of Al-Azhar increased with the arrival of the military rulers in 1952.

Al-Azhar played a greater rule outside Egypt by educating students from Africa and Asia on Islamic sciences and by sending Islamic missionaries and illuminators to many parts of the world.

Al-Azhar could be fairly viewed as **source of Islamic knowledge** for export outside Egypt.

Inside Egypt, Muslim Brothers replaced Al-Azhar by its clandestine style and its ability to adhere to Quranic canons which displease tyrannical rulers. Official Azhar moftis were mostly manipulated to sing the tunes of the ruler.

Exporting of Islamic missionaries and illuminators to remote cultures and nations, by Al-Azhar, have many inadvertent effects. Many of those sent outside Egypt benefited from their **voluntary exiles** by exposure to foreign cultures, they expanded their wisdom and scope on greater world affairs. They also accumulated greater wealth compared to those stayed in Egypt. Thus, many Al-Azhar scholars competed on travel outside Egypt, both to escape the brutal hunting by Egyptian authorities for Islamists and for getting rich.

An Islamic Giant from the twentieth century. Sheikh Muhammad Al-Shaarawy, never dressed western style, sat on the floor with common people, and spoke of Quran in heavenly eloquence.

3.2. Sheikh Muhammad Metwally Al Shaarawy

Like many Egyptian children in rural villages, El-Shaarawy memorized Quran at the age of eleven years. He left the village, travelled to Cairo, to complete his education in Al-Azhar and graduated from Al-Azhar University in 1941 as a teacher of Arabic Language. He was sent to **Saudi Arabia** within Azhar's mission in 1950, 1970, and 1981. In 1963 he served as the Director of the Grand Sheikh of Al-Azhar. In 1966, he traveled to **Algeria** as the head of Al-Azhar Mission and remained for seven years.

Al Shaarawy earned the title of "**The preacher of the century**." He was exceptionally talented in explaining the meanings of the holy Quran in simple words behind the most difficult verses of the Quran. He was indeed the rarest Arabic scholar in the twentieth century by his genius in mastering the Arabic Language in situations formidable to most people.

He could speak to a feared despot or tyrant with total truth without getting the monster to sense the damage of his lasting words.

When Mubarak returned from Ethiopia after a failed attempt to assassinate him, in 1995 AD, Al-Shaarawy met him with the following words:

Arabic Speech

وانى يا سيادة الرئيس اقف على عتبه دنيايا لأستقبل اجل الله فلن اختم حياتي بنفاق ولن ابرز عنتريتي باكتراء ولكني اقول كلمة موجزة للامة كلها حكومتا وحزبا ومعارضة ورجالا وشعب .. اسف ان اقول سلبي .. اريد منهم ان يعلموا ان الملك كله بيدي الله يأتيه من يشاء فلا تأمر لأخذه ولا كيد للوصول إليه فأن الحق سبحانه وتعالى حينما حكي حوار ابراهيم للنمروز ماذا قال له .. الذى حجا ابراهيم فى ربه وهو كافر قال ان اتاه الله الملك فالملك حين ينزله الله قال يأتي الملك لمن يشاء فلا تأمر على الله لملك ولا كيد على الله لحكم لانه لا يحكم احدا فى ملك الله إلا بمراد الله .. فإن كان عادلن فقد نفع بعدله وان كان ظالما بشع الظلم وقبحه فى نفوس كل الناس فيكرهون كل ظالما ولو لم يكن حاكما ولذلك اقول للقوم جميعاً والحمد لله قد تأكد لنا صدق الله فى كلامه بما جاء من الاحداث فكيف كنا نفسر قول الله ويمكرونا ويمكروا الله فكيف نفسروا انهم يكديون كيدا ونكيدوا كيدا الله يريد ان يثبت - قيوميته - على قومه فانا انصح كل من يجول براسه ان يكون حاكما انصحه بان لا تطلبه بل يجب ان تطلب له فان رسول الله قال من طلب من الي شيء اعين عليه ومن طلب شيء وكل إليه .. يا سيادة الرئيس اخر ما احب ان اقوله لك ولعل هذا يكون اخر لقائي انا بك .... (ووضع الشيخ يده على كتفي الرئيس وقال) ... اذا كنت قدرنا فليوفقك الله فإذا كنا قدرك فليعنك الله على ان تتحمل .

English Translation

And I, Mr. President,
I stand at the threshold of my life to receive the verdict of God,
I will not conclude my life in hypocrisy
And I will not emphasize my charisma with prominent calumny,
But I say a brief word for the whole nation, party and opposition, men and people....

Sorry it will be **negative**..

I want them to know that the whole universe is in the hands of God,
He gives it to whom he wishes.

There is no **conspiracy** that could take it (owning the universe)
And no fury to get to it.
The Just Almighty when He narrated the dialogue of Ibrahim to Nimroz

82

What did he say to him? (God talked to Ibrahim)

He who disputed God with Ibrahim when he was **Kafer** (Nimroz was a disbeliever)
He said that he was given the ownership by God.(Nimroz said)

Thus, the ownership when given by God, it comes to whom God wishes.
There is no **conspiracy** that brings it and no **fury** to God for rule.
Because no one rules in the universe of God without God's will.

If he (the ruler) was fair, then he benefits his people.
If he (the ruler) was unjust, then he turns injustice into such **grotesque and ugly trait** in the souls of all people

He (the ruler) turns people to hate every **unjust person**, even if he was not a ruler.

For that reason I wish to tell all people

Thank God, it has been confirmed to us by **what have come from events**

For how can we interpret God's saying?

They (rulers) conned but God conned

For how can we interpret that?

They (rulers) conned conning and we (God) conned conning
And God's conning is designed to fasten his universality on his people.

I advise who has in his mind to become a ruler

I advise him

That he should not ask or demand it
He should be offered (or required to)

Because the messenger of God said

That who is asked to something will be aided on it.
That who asked for something it is assigned to him.

Mr. President

The last thing I would like to tell you,
This may be my last meeting with you (crowd protested the sense of end of a giant Illuminator).

(Sheikh put his hand on President 's shoulders and said) ...

If you were our destiny, then God helps you succeed.
If we were your destiny, then God helps you to bear.

------------ End of Translation ----------

During Mubarak's return from Ethiopia in 1995, after an attempt to assassinate him, Sheikh Muhammad Metwally Al Shaarawy shuns Mubarak (in suit and tie) with a convoluted, abstract, accusation, which Mubarak might have never grasped, and which could confuse any persecutor of Mubarak to trap the old man in charge of cursing the president of Egypt.

Mubarak appeared confused. Al Shaarawy appeared nearing death, shaking, but his words were clear, angry, and very precise.

Even though Anwar Sadat was shot dead by four Islamists empowered with strong beliefs that Sadat must be killed, Al Shaarawy used the same lethal logic without firing bullets.

Al Shaarawy put his hand on Mubarak, scattered the words:

"negative, unjust, grotesque, hated, conspired, fury, conning "

in an obscure confrontation, which he thought might get him arrested, imprisoned, and hung, like Sayyid Qutb's execution by Nasser in 1966.

Mubarak was 14 years in power when he promised earlier to leave power after one term. Mubarak was asked to resign.
AL-Shaarawy attempted his best to move the man's deep conscience.
But, many lives would be lost before Mubarak gave up power on February 11, 2011.

Sheikh Metwally Al Shaarawy never appeared in western dress and took great pride in Arabic language and Islam.

The president of Egypt, Mohamed Morsi squandered the treasures of Egypt on looking and thinking like capitalists.

The contrast between a simple sheikh with great knowledge of his religion and heritage and the president with shallow education and great arrogance parallels the contrast between the revolting people and the ruling few.

3.3. Sheikh Mahmoud Shaaban

Sheikh **Mahmoud Shaaban** of Al-Azhar University claimed that contemporary muslims are the lousiest merchants who have the precious pearls of Islam but fail to sell them to needy buyers.

Islam avoided the illogical dilemma of Christianity of making God takes the form of Jesus, using Jesus as a power to save, love, and do magic. Additionally, Islam set rules for wars, marriage, and social interactions that comprise actions, retributions, and rewards that parallel modern systems of civilized governments.

Young, aggressive, well-trained on Quranic Rhetoric, Sheikh Mahmoud Shaaban is a signature of the rise of Salafi muslims in Egypt. His TV channel was closed after ousting Morsi. He advanced the clear thought that:

"If Morsi is removed, we will never have a president."

Shaaban's greatest joke is: **"Bring Me A Man"**, as he always asks any interviewing TV station not to let woman in his presence.

Shaaban appears neurotic, always moving, always shouting, and never docile, except when he was ambushed in crowds by hostile youths, mostly fascinating with his eloquence, though apparently threatening to hurt him.

Shaaban was viewed as hero and savior because of his relentless offenses. When confronted by another sheikh who works for the government and who claimed that dancing, singing, and exposure of women were gifts of expression of **"Biaan"**, Shaaban launched vicious attacks on those whom he perceived as distorter of Quran.

Apparently, our sheikh and professor Mahmoud Shaaban fell in the trap of localizing Quran to his immediate misery, rather than viewing the grand universe. Like the saying **"misery loves company"**, Shaaban projects his constricted style on others. On the issue of dancing and singing, Shaaban rejected the idea that dancing and singing were heavenly **gifts of expression**.

It might be true that in most parts of the world, dancers and singers suffer enormously in gaining stable employment or living stable family life. Also, both professions require extensive training and talent that far exceed standardized education. But, for Shaaban, shaking body parts or playful singing were distraction from God's canons of discipline and restraint.

If fact, Sheik Shaaban's young age and limited life exposure explain his firm adherence of mainstream conservative interpretation of Quran. He views pleasing the masses with any thing

86

other than his own clownish lecturing as deviation from the straight path of God. To his credit, those fell in the traps of singing and dancing, without alternative intellectual achievements, faced grave outcomes which many families do not wish their children to face.

Most dancers, singers, and professional athletes lived in the underworld of illicit drugs and crimes. In this book, we narrated the murders of Soad Hosny and Suzanne Tamim. Both women were kind, naïve, generous human beings on the personal level. They resorted to performance to make living. The Egyptian poet Ahmed Fouad Negm explains the days preceding the murder of Soad Hosny. He described her as an angel with the greatest heart a woman could have. Negm shouted on Hosny when he knew that she fell in the traps of **Abdulatif El-Menawy**. Negm alerted Hosny that El-Menawy was an informant of National Security Police and he would be after the secrets that Hosny has on many state-officials. Soad Hosny was murdered shortly after.

3.4. Sheikh Ahmed Al- Tayyib

Ahmed Al- Tayyib, the present Mofti of Al-Azhar issued Fatwa to criminalize the rioters against Mubarak, in 2011.

Two years latter, on July 3, 2013, Al-Tayyib showed up with Pope Tawadros of the Coptic Egyptian Church to endorse El-Sissi's coup.

Al-Tayyib announced his lack of knowledge of the massacre of Rabaa Al-Adawyia, but did not hesitate to describe the arrested and imprisoned Muslim Brothers as cowards, misleading the people, and trading with Islam.

Inside Egypt, all Azhar's Sheiks and Professors favored safety over God's canons and encouraged tyrants to execute their plunders and massacres.

Outside Egypt, only those in Qatar, which helped ignite the Arab Spring, were encouraged to scream and shout with the name of God and Quran. Wagdi Ghoneim and Yusuf Al-Qaradawi are among those Qatar-based Islamists.

Inside Egypt, all known or outspoken Muslim Brothers were shut off by imprisonment, torture, and execution.

3.5. Sheikh Ali Goumaa

Sheikh, Professor **Ali Goumaa**, the ex-mofti of Al-Azhar distorted all noble values in Quran, advised the Egyptian army and police to **shoot to kill**, described the civilian protesters against the coup as rotten, cockroaches, un-Egyptians, unworthy to live.

Goumaa was a strange aberration in the history of Egypt. His use of slang words and overzealous appeasement of Mubarak and El-Sissi tainted the mission of Al-Azhar which stood to previous despots and invaders according the highest moral values of Quran.

Sheikh, Professor, and Mofti Al-Azhar, Ali Goumaa sets a new record for the **Sheikh of the Coup**.

Goumaa distorted the Quran and Hadeeth by telling the coup generals that the Angels and Prophet Muhammad will be with them, that the protesters are rotten.

Calls for suing Goumaa for encouraging massacres started as soon his speech was sneaked out.

The three top generals who invited Ali Goumaa to speak in military gathering are blamed for allowing a crazy sheikh to speak profanity, distort Quran, and tell lies.

Lt. Gen. **Sedki Sobhi** covers his mouth as he displayed similar signs of unease in previous situation.

The other two generals, Ibrahim (left to center) and El-Sissi (center) show little emotion from this delinquent sheikh, playing the game of appeasing the coup generals, in comical and irritating manner.

That leaked video raised widespread criticism in Egypt and the Islamic world.

CHAPTER 4

Muslim Brotherhood

4.1. Clandestine Work

In 1928, the poorest villages of Egypt overcame the trouble of travel to the Capital of Egypt, where Al-Azhar University was located, by creating their own self-established religious school of the Muslim Brothers. (Today, Al-Azhar has colleges in many providences beside Cairo.)

Like most Egyptian villages in those days, peasants lived in self sufficiency. Most children had no birth certificates, married people needed no marriage certificates, youth could evade military conscription, and dead people were buried without death certificates.

Thus, Muslim Brothers were born outside the tutelage of the state. They needed no complicated registration procedures. They chose members based on very close personal relationships. They interacted immediately with their relatives and neighbors in education, health care, sheltering, marriage, and death.

Thus, Muslim Brotherhood avoided the morbid constraints imposed on Al-Azhar institution.

4.2. Islamic Project

4.2.1. Islamic mindset

The supreme power of the human mind is recognized by all religions as the cradle of reality. Man **thinks** and **acts** by the work of minds, which have been the main focus of Islam in defining and managing good and evil. Therefore, the main ideas implanted by Quran in the mind of muslims define the individual and group's present and future actions.

In particular, the future of Egypt will be influenced mainly by the Quranic judgment that the wicked must be fought or killed, until they repent and the ordained laws of the Lord are upheld.

With millions of Egyptians impoverished by few thugs on the higher seats of power in Egypt, greater **class wars,** from within man's mind, are inevitable, in the process of national survival.

A quick survey of the Quranic ideas (in **suras** or chapters of Quran) shows the essence of power of faith in defining the future of Egypt.

1. Surat **Al-Fatiha** (The Opening) emphasizes guidance to the **straight path**.

2. Surat **Al-Baqara** (The Cow) emphasizes guidance to the **pious and righteous** persons who adhere to the words of Quran.

3. Surat **Al-Imran** (The House of Imran) emphasizes guidance to **right and wrong** and the Lord's retribution and rewards.

4. Surat **An-Nisa** (Women) emphasized the **mutual rights** of sexes and the honor of kinship.

5. Surat **Al-Maeda** (The Table) describes **forbidden** and **permitted** brands of food which mankind should abstain from or consume.

6. Surat **Al-Anaam** (Livestock) emphasizes the relationship between society and the source of **sustenance** of life on earth.

7. **Al-Araf** (The Heights) defines the **good** and **bad** powers of the human psyche.

8. **Al-Anfal** (Spoils of war) outlines the rules of dealing with **defeated enemy**.

9. **Al-Tawba** (Repentance) describes the condition of **fighting evil liars** and **infidels**.

10. **Yunus** (Jonah) defines the meaning of **divine revelation**.

11. **Hud** (Hud) describes the meaning of **monolithic God**.

12. **Yusuf** (Joseph) emphasized the immense power of caring for **orphaned humans** who could turn into imminent men.

13. **Al-Rad** (The Thunder) counts the endless **natural factors** that made life livable.

14. **Ibrahim** (Abrahim) emphasized the role of **security in place and mind**.

114. **An-Nas** (Mankind) describes mankind as a mix of **good** and **bad** actors.

In short, Quran aligns all human **moral compasses** towards one God of one heavenly system of canons of justice, equality, and good deeds.

That suffices to explain the morbid resentment of **military rulers,** who lack either the Quranic conviction or the shrewdness of educated and learned individuals. Even though **Gamal Abdul Nasser** was the most beloved military officer in Egypt's history, Nasser's severe deviation from the spirit of Islam handed Egypt to military officers. Those ended with the country in bleak socioeconomic situation.

In fact, Nasser was a complete aberration in the history of Egypt, a man who never aspired to get rich, loved his nation more than he realized, resigned his job as soon as he sensed his error, and changed the world map of Africa, Asia, and Latin America by his keen sense that **he was sent to save the poor from the injustice of the rich**.

The presence of **Muslim Brotherhood** and other Islamic factions cannot be ignored from the political process in Egypt because of the dwindling trend of **secular doctrines** in administering justice in impoverished populations.

4.2.2. Western mindset
In the west, civil legal trials consume on average between five to ten years if judges do not abuse the summary dismissal. In Egypt, some cases linger over 20 years in court. With a nation

suffering from increasing homeless people contrasted by increasing number of billionaires, Quranic justices thrust to replace secular injustices.

The stumbling course of the **islamic project** cannot be separated from the prevalent fictional conception of Islam by many detached leading Islamic figures.

What facts make Islam the long and lasting competitor for western secularism?

Secularism brought vast spreading moral and social decay in western nations, rendering mass riots the only method of rectifying social injustice. Meanwhile, complacent and moody judicial systems are derived mainly by a class of fraternal judges promoting their own social philosophies and designs.

In the United States, the **Thirteenth Amendment** was enacted in 1865 AD to abolish slavery and authorize Congress to enforce abolition. In 1870 AD, the **Fifteenth Amendment** was also enacted to prohibit the federal government and the states from using a citizen's race, color, or previous status as a slave as a qualification for voting. Women were not allowed to vote until 1920 after the **Nineteenth Amendment** was enacted.

The fundamental doctrine in western systems of justice is the **cost of administering justice**, not the consequences of inflecting injustice on voiceless citizens. A defendant who could not afford the high cost of good attorney will have greater chances of losing his or her freedom or even life. A wealthy defendant could purchase his freedom with money.

The famous trial in the twentieth century, in the USA, of **O.J. Simpson** demonstrates the ineffectiveness of American system of justice. Simpson was vindicated from double murder crime in 1995 when he was wealthy enough to hire the most famous criminal attorneys in the country. Twelve years latter, Simpson was imprisoned for life in a case of robbery, when he ran out of cash to hire attorneys of the stature a wealthy criminal could get.

An American federal judge explained that a defendant who could afford a highly paid attorney should get better justice than a defendant who cannot hire an effective attorney. He likened that by medical or dental care. Thus, costly counselor service is equivalent to better **administration of justice**.

How such injustice in western civilization repulses muslims from secularism?

Due to past experience with colonialism, most Islamic nations attribute their governments' corruption to the **influence of western powers.** The USA is perceived as the Great Satan that replaced past British colonialism. The new generations of those nations learned the hard lesson that they must invent their own system of government, independent of western philosophies.

Hence, the treasures of Islamic heritage are resurrected and refined in such manner that Islam could avert the massive injustice inflicted on people by economically driven western secular judicial system.

Despite the **two millennia of Christianity**, only in 1964 that the first black girl **Ruby Nell Bridges Hall** was allowed to attend all-white elementary school in the South, and under the protection of federal armed forces. She attended William Frantz Elementary School, at 3811 North Galvez Street, New Orleans, Louisiana, 70117, United States.

Mohamed ElBaradie, the Nobel Prize winner for peace, was rejected by the majority of Egyptians for his endorsement of the **American liberal ideals**. Those are viewed as lacking all sensitivities to the dire needs of the poor. The 6-year old black child Ruby Hall needed three federal marshals to protect her from white attackers.

ElBaradie volunteered an explanation of Islam as a religion no different from others and that Islam should not be used in governing Egypt. That wise thought of **separating state from religion** aligned ElBaradie with the Great Satan, and led to deeper and microscopic inspection of the ElBaradie's wish-washy views. Those were perceived to turn Egypt into another American failing society of material gratification minus the moral empathy for the poor majority.

In the shadows of western secularism implemented in Egyptian system of government, the impoverished and poorly educated fill prisons. The mitigating circumstances of **civil inequality** that led to unjust poverty and illiteracy are ignored in dealing with social ills.

Such apathy towards civil injustice could be tolerated in affluent western societies, not so in Egypt. In most Islamic nations, the vast majority of the population is voiceless and chronically oppressed.

Most third-world immigrants to western societies return home with the lasting impression **that economically driven judicial system** deprives humanity from its moral and ethical dignity, empowers the wealthy and connected, thus leaving great segments of society permanently oppressed and isolated.

For one, most court trials require as long as 5 years to get underway, if the judges were honest enough to avoid the abused summary dismissal. Dismissals are most of times affirmed by review courts. Thus, not only that the length of time to administer justice is ridiculously unjust for impoverished population, but also the belief and bias of judges determine the outcome of administering justice.

The arrival of the fast, affordable, and global **electronic communication** in the form of internet and mobile cell phones penetrated the state-imposed censorship on transfer of information, thus allowing most muslims to get closer look into the chaos of secular western social structure. Under the banner of state law, all forms of social ills have been empowered by the fact that judicial resolution of deceptive practices can be easily frustrated by financial attrition such that judicial resources lag behind spread of social ills.

Gambling and prostitution outpaced judicial resources by briberies and lobbying. Pornography sneaked under the cover of artistic performance and freedom of expression. Worse of all, students are flooded by fiction literature based solely of personal creativity, while excluding any religious figurative fiction despite its purposeful intention.

4.2.3. Stumbling Course

The stumbling course of the islamic project is not only attributed to fictional beliefs of its followers, but also to the profound propaganda of **Christian western** Society that decided that religion and government cannot mix.

Yet, all those who run western governments go to churches, temples, or were raised in such religious backgrounds and cannot claim to be able to separate their beliefs from their decisions. For one reason, beliefs are not amenable to definitive tests. For another, all government and judicial decisions are given sovereign immunity that prohibits citizens from repealing fraudulent judicial decisions.

In fact, both states and US Supreme Courts do not accept more than 2% of **appeals for review**. That gives the lower courts of appeal plenty of room to deviate from decisions of supreme courts with impunity.

Thus, the secular western judicial systems inherit its morbid basis of injustice by balancing justice with **cost of litigation**, and turning blind eye to the unseen ills that accumulate when injustice and apathy towards the suffering of individuals constitute the norms of western justice.

Islamists are overcome by the sweeping propaganda that **religion divides people,** leads to unreal and detached planning unsuitable for governing people.

On that front, islamists could succeed by exclusion, where previous secular governments plundered Egypt to the rock bottom. Hence, a bearded, front-face tattooed islamists look more like people unwilling to steal or plunder a nation for life. Yet also here lies the greatest danger against islamists by vast section of secular capitalists and military and police officers thrive on the oldest trades of drugs, guns, prostitution, nepotism, and bribery. Those have already managed to spoil Morsi's rule.

In contrast, the beneficiaries from the high moral agenda of islamists are the unarmed and impoverished population. Those could only riot, protest, and passively and aggressively impede progress in society without the decisive power to functioning and to progressive governments.

While attempting to advance the islamic project, most islamists make the fatal error of conveying **Allah** as a speaker and living master somewhere in heavens who has already set his rules in the Quranic scripture, thus obviating the need for others to think, refine, or criticize on the basis that Allah's words are not amenable to argumentation.

What went wrong? Is there future for the Islamic Project?

It will be shown in this book that **Egyptian islamists** were overcome by the vast secular, heavily armed and poorly educated military and police soldiers.

Those overpowered the shrewdness and wisdom of Islam, enlisted the willing and bribed media agencies to run their propaganda machine while the entire state of Egypt was crippled by emergency law and curfew, the national train transportation was suspended, and widespread violence gripped the nation in unprecedented chaos.

A veiled muslim Egyptian woman described the state of the media as follows:
"Give me immoral media demagogues; I give you ill-informed citizens"

Good words of islamists were trumped by snipers and gunfire in dramatic fashion that exceeded any theatrical provocative **violent massacres**. Gun shots that explode inside the bodies of the victims scattered their guts and interiors. Civilians are gunned down by hidden snipers without giving escape access or warning time. Government failed to convince people of its intent to use lethal power or concerted effort to burn and hide murdered civilians.

All massacres are attributed the **failure of islamists** to adhere to the spirit of Islam of combining military power with Islamic teaching in the manner Prophet Muhammad did in confronting Kouraish, fourteen centuries ago.

Somehow, Muslim Brothers bought into the idea of unarmed protest and democratic process and ended up being arrested under the power of guns, all democratically elected islamists were locked up with fabricated charges by the military officers. Those turned the government into private business.

4.3. Falling with Grace

Muslim Bothers triumphed in democratic election yet ended up with its leaders back in prisons.

This is the historic comedy of Abdul Fattah El-Sissi.

El-Sissi took the oath of duty in front of the newly elected president Mohamed Morsi. Within one year, El-Sissi plotted to oust Morsi, restore Mubarak's old regime, appoint a temporary president **Adly Mansour**, took the oath again in front of Adly Mansour, then stumbled on the escalating massacres he ordered and executed. Those posed the inevitable fate of his execution if he lost grip on the military. At 6000 murdered civilians on the hands of El-Sissi's men, he asked frankly for immunity before he could give up his military post to run for president. As a military general, he cannot be tried for his crimes in civilian courts. Thus, **the hunter is being hunted.**

President Mohamed Morsi committed his worst mistake by removing those two top generals, **Mohamed Tantawi** (middle) and **Sami Anan** (left).

The two men were too old to look for rivalry with him. Their removal and replacement by 56-year old El-Sissi led to the latter ousting Morsi, both for revenge for his uniformed generals and for his own ambition. Thus, the naivety of Morsi and his lack of experience in street fighting and back-stabbing got him stabbed in the back.

Barack Obama chose an older vice president **Joe Biden**, **George W. Bush** chose an older vice president **Dick Cheney**, both for the purpose of avoiding subordinate rival.

The rural, naïve, academic, and Islamist Mohamed Morsi did what the Egyptian comedian **Younis Shalabi** would have done: dumb mistakes. Mohamed Morsi was likened by Younis Shalabi's role of a dumb villager lost in the lights of busy metropolitan Cairo.

Three exceptional intellectuals of the Islamic Project.

Safwat Hegazy (left) was the most beloved Salafi muslim known for famous statement: "Morsi is a red-line, anyone who touches Morsi, we will spray him by blood."

Essam Elerian (middle) the God-Father of the Islamic Project and the most out-spoken and educated Muslim Brother, well-known for his deep faith in Quran and his referral to Quranic verses in all aspects of politics and life. Elerian was the only top Islamist who evaded capture by El-Sissi's regime.

Mohamed Beltagy (right) is another heavy-weight Muslim Brother, whose daughter **Asma Beltagy** (cover photo) was shot dead on August 14, 2013, by El-Sissi's solders in Rabaa El-Adawiya during the civilian protest against the military coup.

Asma Beltagy, the daughter of Mohamed Beltagy, was shot dead on August 14, 2013, by El-Sissi's solders in Rabaa El-Adawiya during the civilian protest against the military coup.

The news of murder of this 16-year old girl put tears in the eyes of Tayyib Erdoğan, the Prime Minister of Turkey. Her death rebuts the lies of Sheikh Ahmed El-Tayyib, the mofti of Azhar, that islamists do not sacrifice their own and lure others to death.

Even though two thousand civilians, men, women, children, and elderly were slaughtered in Rabaa Al-Adawiya and Nahda's massacres, the death of Asma Al-Beltagy was a symbol of a historic massacre which will alter the history of Egypt forever.

Egyptian islamists did not grasp the lessons of the **Iranian Islamic revolution** of 1979 or the **Algerian Islamic Revolution** of 1992. In Iran, Imam Khomeini's charismatic personality altered the course of Iran's contemporary history by uniting Iranians to expel the Shah, dismantle his brutal regime, stand against outside aggression from **Iraq** backed by the West and neighboring oil nations.

In contrast to Iran, **Algeria's Islamic movement** faced so many difficulties. Algeria's Islamic leaders, including **Abbas Madani** and the following leader **Ali bil-Haaj**, lacked the required characteristics of influential leaders, they failed in their efforts to unite all Algerian muslims under the umbrella of their leadership.

In the late 1980s and early 1990s, Algeria took concrete steps toward the establishment of a liberal democracy. The regime assumed that the electorate would rally behind its newly found political liberalism. As is the case in Egypt, the **Front Islamique du Salut** won the initial round of municipal elections and set to win national round of voting scheduled for 1992.

However, the Algerian National Assembly election was not allowed to run, the army intervened on January 11, 1992 to unseat President **Chadli Benjadid** and call off the electoral proceedings, thus pushing Algeria into a civil war of savagery and violence. The struggle was marked by massacres of civilians, including the notorious 1997 killings by radical islamists of some four hundred women, children, and men at **Bentalha** in the Mitidja plain. The Algerian conflict has claimed perhaps 100,000 lives.

In both cases of failures to establish Islamic governments in Algeria and Egypt, the **deep secular states** (comprising of illegitimately enriched cronies of previous tyrants funded and planned police, military, and non-uniformed proxy militia) impeded all economic activities and

101

developments. By squeezing the life out of 90 million already impoverished Egyptians, anarchy ensued. They placed the public in dire straits of unemployment, hungers, and severe shortage of necessities of survival.

Mohamed Morsi explained in his last speech how the deep state was funded by **thirty wealthy Egyptian families**. He accused them for dumping the gasoline in the desert to cause shortage of fuel, interrupting the national electric network, hiding wheat and flour to prevent access to the bakeries, and sabotaging the train transportation safety procedure.

Mohammad Hassanien Heikal was one of those suddenly enriched billionaires, known as "**the philosopher of the military coup**". Heikal complained that Egypt was madly penetrated by foreign agencies on all fronts. In fact, Heikal was contracted by **Al-Jazeera** as a long time expert on Egyptian politics since 1940's, was later dismissed by the Qatar's funded TV station, re-contracted by a pro-government station.

Heikal advocated banning AL-Jazeera from broadcasting in Egypt. An advocacy that was carried out by the El-Sissi. He ordered arresting, expelling, and imprisoning the employees of Al-Jazeera and instructed the Egyptian Army to interfere with satellite frequencies of Al-Jazeera.

The two assets conferred by Islam and Quran aided the Muslim Brothers to sail through the pending **military coup** with exceptional grace unprecedented in the history of reverse revolution.

Until the last moment Mohamed Morsi refrained from making foolish decisions such assassinating his opponents or ordering aggressive suppression of the opposing riots. Even the belligerent **Black Bloc**, which caused destruction and violent aggressions concealed under masks, were left to the police and courts. Those never acted against such extreme violation of any civilized nation.

Morsi let rioters throw Molotov and use bulldozers to break through the presidential palace. He and his team implemented the best of Islam in **falling out of power** without criminal errors, while letting the coup leaders engage in the most blatant violation of law that could easily lead to their execution.

Not that Mohamed Morsi plotted to fall with grace, but that grace was Morsi's life-long pursuit which blinded him to the pending coup.

Morsi married his cousin in order to avert family instability, focus on academic ambitions, advance his Islamic utopian dreams, and spare his family the pains of leaving a daughter unmarried.

El-Sissi resorted to the military to avoid reading, study, or uncertain employment challenges in uncertain market. Like most military persons, the absence of the father from family life and meager academic depth of the military contribute to unstable family of military people.

El-Sissi' shameless transgression on the law and Morsi's restraints for doing harms were expected outcome from their social makeup.

Even though islamists appear to have lost power, they brilliantly relieved themselves from the **impasse of economic failure** created long before their arrival to power. As the latest prime minister of Egypt **Omar Suleiman** stated on February 3, 2011, that all sources of national income have been dropped by the third due to the riots.

Despite the fact that Suleiman never told truth, fabricated every fact to support Mubarak, the Egyptian economy has collapsed long time before **2011's revolution**.

Gunmen Open Fire On Praying Muslims In Egypt City of Arish, July 5, 2013

| Muslim crowd in praying | Chaos after and during firing |

| Injured falled | Retrun to rescue fallen fellows |

In the Bedouin culture of Sinai's Arabs, firing on praying crowds by the military is one among many stupid decisions taken by the coup leaders of Egypt.

Mohamed Morsi calmed down Sinai by addressing the needs of the Sinai's Bedouins. Most of those were unjustly convicted by the Egyptian courts, imprisoned, and deprived from basic human rights. The ousting of Mohamed Morsi and the Islamists by El-Sissi meant armed Jihad in Sinai was inevitable.

4.4. The battle of Wits

Al-Arabyia TV

Al-Jazeera TV

The two foreign TV stations in Egypt; **Al-Arabiya and Al-Jazeera,** competed on the coverage of the Arab Spring. Al-Jazeera was accused as the mastermind of anarchy in the Middle East. **Ahmed Mansour** and **Khadega Ben Qena** from Al-Jazeera competed with **Mahmoud Al-Warwary** and **Muntaha Al-Romhy** from Al-Arabiya.

Mansour is self-declared Muslim Brother, combined the model of the American commentator **Ted Koppel** with the graceful smile and humor of Islam. The frozen and dry outlook of Koppel is substituted by Mansour's flexible and combative persona. Similarly, the fanatic bias of Koppel to Jews parallels Mansour's fanatic bias to Muslims.

Even though Qatar is more liberal and westernized than Saudi Arabia, Khadega Ben Qena switched her western dress to the Muslim attire. Oppositely, Muntaha Al-Romhy from the Arabian based Al-Arabiya adopted the provocative western fashion.

From within, some saboteur inadvertently opened the camera on Muntaha Al-Romhy prior to the broadcast, showing her anxiety about makeup and hairstyling. The same 1991's joke made by **Ross Perot** about Presidential runners Bush and Clinton for their obsession with makeup over their ability to govern. Muntaha Al-Romhy lends support to the Islamic tradition of confident women living for purpose and characters, not physical beauty and artificial makeup. Not that Muntaha Al-Romhy was less attractive than Khadega Ben Qena, but because anxiety and obsession about physical attraction places great burden on family, children, and husband when the mother or daughter is drained in physical obsession.

Who would the listener believe? A western looking Muntaha Al-Romhy or an Islamic looking Khadega Ben Qena? A western dressed Mahmoud Al-Warwary or a bearded and eyed glass wearing Ahmed Mansour?

Mansour delivered the Ted Koppel's objective stabbing critics mellowed by the eastern cheerful face. In addition, Mansour parted his country, turned to international citizen, thus evaded Egyptian oppression. **Khadega** showed a changing Muslim determined to honor her roots, swam against the stream, in media culture long accused for liberal decay. Khadega also parted Tunisia, turned into international citizen, thus also evaded her country's government oppression. **Mahmoud Al-Warwary** worked in his birth place, ended up bowing to the Egyptian Pharaoh. **Muntaha Al-Romhy** brought the alien western style of women educated in Britain into the Islamic world, remained unconscious to the Islamic mindset.

Nothing aided in marketing the two foreign TV stations as **believability**. Al-Jazeera conveyed the pulse of the streets and the souls of the people. Al-Arabiya fabricated and fell in the traps of the west in a culture that rejects every western folly.

Hence, Al-Arabiya aligned with thirty four Egyptian TV stations, all broadcasting the military agenda of the coup. Al-Jazeera was banned and its employees in Egypt were hunted and imprisoned.

CHAPTER 5

Divine Science

5.1. Doer, Death, Deeds

Among the most notorious thinkers who abuse the schism of physical sciences from humanitarian sciences is Mohamed Hassanien Heikal. Heikal spared no time criticizing Mohamed Morsi for being **material engineer**, not humanitarian scientist. Also, Morsi facilitated Heikal's job by claiming to know scientists and to be one of them.

Heikal's ingenious plundering of Egypt was seasoned since the 1940's. Heikal worked with three military rules, none of whom has **physical or humanitarian scientific** background. In addition, Heikal knew well that Islamists were the most educated intellectuals in Egypt, not only in the villages, clinics, mosques, market, but also in foreign nations.

Among many of Muslim Brother escapees was **Youssef Moustafa Nada**, the noted businessman and financial strategist. Nada started from making and selling cheese in the 1960's, in Alexandria, Egypt, to becoming a billionaire and king of cement in the world. Nada's fortune started when Nasser persecuted Muslim Brothers. He fled to Libya during its years as a kingdom. From there, he found his way to Switzerland where he lived and prospered to great wealth.

Muslim Brother and the 'King of Cement' **Youssef Moustafa Nada.**

Bridging the schism between material and spiritual sciences is clearly demonstrated in the pillars of physical sciences. Isaac Newton erected physical sciences on the biblical concept that matter represents death, or **inertia,** which requires force for motion.

Newton's first law of inertia embodies the very core of faith.

No life can ensue without force.

What is source of force?

That is the same question:

Who created God?

Newton's pragmatic mindset deserted such pursuit for the origin of God and worked his way through the creatures of God.

If force moves dead matter (or inert matter or inertia), then there must be a canon that governs such effect. Newton proposed the biblical rule of **deeds and rewards**.

The amount of motion is proportional to the amount of force.

That is Newton's second law. It stated that the amount of inertia (or mass) and the acceleration of the mass must be proportional to the amount of force.

To complete briefing the Bible, Newton adopted the rule of **rewards and retribution**.

Newton's third law designated **equal and opposite reaction to every reaction**.

Every field of science, humanitarian or physical, is founded on such basic doctrine:

Doer, Death, and Deeds

Or

Death, Change, and Equilibrium

No dead state can be changed without force, and change must result in equilibrium of living state, such that actions are opposed by equal reactions.

The doctrine of logic and reason implies that every **effect** must have a **cause**. But, no scientist can delve into causation without knowing the limits of such pursuit. Also, every scientist is limited within the scope of life or equilibrium between actions and reactions, or rewards and retributions.

5.2. Celestial Design

The widely perceived potency of the **scientific method** eludes many people to believe that science is the safest alternative to religion.

The material gains from technology and the fast and constantly evolving advances in material sciences impose their lure on unwary people. Most dismiss the basic role of mental rapport and living in **peace with nature**.

My first introduction to study of psychiatry under Professor **Ali El-Garem**, in the University of Alexandria, faculty of Medicine, in 1978, El-Garem stressed the fact that 70% of all medical diseases are psychiatric in origin. To support his lectures with clinical cases, Professor Al-Garem prepared very vivid and simple cases which medical students could easily perform the diagnosis and differential diagnosis without great difficulties.

A case of a wife presented by left-side hemi-paresis, entailing paralysis on the entire left side of her body, had history of previous diagnosis by medical and surgical doctors, with protracted laboratory imaging and blood analysis. The patient's history and clinical presentation immediately led to the psychiatric cause of the patient's paralysis. That was neither anatomical nor organic lesion, but mental dysfunction.

Beside that narrow reflection on the mental control of motor functions, such as moving limbs, organs, or control circulation, the **cerebral functions** comprise a bona fide mystery of nature.

All human conflicts and wars, battles, and politics devised to resolve those conflicts are products of our reasoning, or cerebral functions.

Since the seventeenth century, the most prominent German mathematician of that era, **Johannes Kepler** worked as the astronomer and astrologer for the Emperor for his astrological wit.

Even though Kepler was never credited for any substantial contribution to astrology, his experimental observations of celestial motion led to Kepler's famous three laws of planetary motion: **Ellipses**, **Equal Areas**, and **Harmonies**.

For the first time in history of mankind, man learned that all planets travel in elliptical orbits around their star. Kepler never doubted that **God's hands** must be found in such impeccable design of the universe.

Kepler discovered the other two laws of equal areas swept by planets and the laws of planetary rotational periods. Since 1630 AD to date, no human could figure out the source of **gravitational force** other than attributing that to the inertial content of matter.

How could Kepler relate the celestial motion of planets to the ailing health of the Emperor?

Kepler's findings fall far beyond the known science of his time. Kepler died in 1630, a dozen years before the birth of Isaac Newton in 1642.

By 1670's, Isaac Newton confronted the great dilemma created by Kepler's three laws of planetary motions. Newton could reason well within the laws of the **Bible** that **God alone could bring the dead to life, and God alone could change life**. Thus, God's inertia, force, and change do not accommodate Kepler's laws.

Frustrated that the **God of the Bible** cannot help in explaining how planets spin in their orbits, Newton proposed the universal law of gravitation.

Thus, while Kepler died believing that **God must have hands** in pulling the planets and stars according to three well-known laws. Newton suggested that God's hands reside in the materials of the celestial objects. The greater the material contents of celestial objects, the greater is their pulling or gravitational effect.

There would be another three centuries before Kepler's observations be put to use in many branches of physical sciences and be known as the **conservation of angular momentum**. Only in 1909, **Niels Bohr** found great help in Kepler's law when he attempted to account for the electronic shells in the atomic structure.

Bohr reasoned that electrons must rotate in fixed orbits around the nucleus in the same manner that planets rotate around the stars and without planets falling into the star or electrons getting sucked in by the nucleus.

Not that Bohr's model stood the test of time, which it did not, or that Kepler's laws were applicable to subatomic physics. Both men, Kepler and Bohr, stuck to the pragmatic principle that **the ultimate actor must be reached in steps** that would take many centuries or generations.

Why do celestial objects or subatomic entities adhere to precise laws?

As science struggles with the common challenges in physical sciences, humanitarian sciences bear immediate and urgent effects on man's survival.

Civilization is founded on man's exception **gift of intellect**.

In Islam, mankind must conform to precise laws of heavens, not different from those imposed on celestial and subatomic particles. Thus, all people are equal in front of one supreme power based solely on their **deeds.**

It might be true that a killer could inflict grave insults on others, given some chance to live, either by choice or by design. It is also true that some killers are more influential than others, depending on their social and political clouts, and some has killed millions of innocent people, yet went unpunished.

How do the canons of the Divine serve his creatures?

This question is also applicable to physical sciences, as any law of nature requires meticulous effort by man in order to benefit from natural resources.

For example, the discovery of antibiotics in the 1940's spared the lives of millions of people from infectious diseases. Before such discovery by scientists, many millions of infected people died unduly due to man's ignorance or lack of knowledge of such scientific canon of antibiotics.

Thus, the divine laws cannot implement themselves nor **there is a physical divine that could do the work of man for man.**

Yet, the necessity of divine canons parallels the necessity of physical laws of nature. Quranic canons emphasize **the inner working of mind** that accompanies the person in conscious and sleep states, every moment of living. Physical laws facilitate the control of man over the resources of nature.

The gains from conforming to physical and moral canons of Quran are comprised of individual and social contracts according to which the individual and the community are bonded by well defined guidelines.

5.3. Darwin's Origin of Species

The closest science could get to explain the purpose or origin in life is **the theory of evolution**, which originally appeared in 1859 A.D. as "The Origin of Species" by Charles Darwin.

As many fields of science integrated on many fronts, the discovery of the DNA added greater practicality and credibility to the Darwin's views. However, as expected, the **origin of species** was the wrong description to Darwin's theory, because nothing in science could predict origin or end of universal processes.

Darwin succeeded or had the courage to oppose the figurative canons of the Bible and described the obvious **anatomical pattern** of creatures. Darwin's major downfall was his total inability to carve any logical scenario to the evolution of the human mind.

Of course, **chaos** and **chance** alone cannot account for the origin of ordered design of biological system, nor could biological systems rising out of chaos and chance learn or incline or intend to favor survival over decay.

Ironically, **Charles Darwin** attempted to apply the same anatomical pattern of continuous spectral variation among species onto the spectral variation on mental cerebration. To Darwin, the individuals inhabiting remote places of the globe were less evolved than a European individual living in highly structured society.

Meanwhile, Prophet Muhammad was undoubtedly born and grew in the most impoverished and remote part of Arabian Peninsula. In the seventh century, the means of transportation were camels and horses when Europe slipped in **Dark Ages**. However, the words of Muhammad and his rituals have captivated the minds of billions of his followers for fourteen centuries.

Muhammad tackled the most elusive aspects of life of creation, creator, moral mechanics, and divine canons of rewards and retributions.

Darwin limited his book to the anatomical pattern of species yet accused man for ignorance for assuming that a higher creator stands behind the diversity of species. Darwin attributed such **diversity** to chaos and chance such that the fittest can ride the tide of chaos and adapt to its forces, the unfit perishes.

Darwin's theory was shielded by the serious failure of **Christianity** in offering reasonable or compelling interpretation of creation. The adherence of Christianity to a magical God, born to a mother without a father, never wrote the Bible but let his Holy Ghost inspire others to do so, all rendered Christianity unbearable to objective minds.

The Christian teachings that Jesus was lift to heaven, died for our sins, did miracles and still can do miracles despite his death, also placed Christianity among the ranks of superstitious beliefs, not conducive to intellectual objectivity.

In contrast to Christianity, Muhammad was born and died as human, rejected magic and miracles, married and fathered children, fought wars, lost some, won others.

Muhammad earned credibility for developing Quran over twenty years, starting at age of forty. By any modern scientific criteria, Muhammad's age at the inception of Quran corresponds perfectly to the age of maturity of a messenger capable of leading a tribe, a nation, or mankind to a designated moral path.

Not only that Jesus died at the age of thirty one, when a man could not have been able to accumulate the intellectual maturity to establish sound moral doctrine, but also that all Christian authorities attribute the biblical contents to Jesus' soul, not to his actual human intellect.

It is even harder for muslims to reject Darwin's theory in the view that Quran encourages scientific curiosity, ranks men of knowledge and curiosity above others, and declares that man could never know the laws of nature without the divine's will.

The view that Darwin's evolution contradicts the canons of the divine lacks any credence. Quranic verses were inspired by Muhammad, who never claimed to know or master the laws of nature, acknowledged the missions of all previous prophets, from Ibrahim, Moses, to Jesus.

In fact, Muhammad's main thrust is "**Biaan**" or revelation of God's glory in inspiring his servants and messengers to guide their followers to straight paths. Muhammad never advocated that Quran was a book of facts or that muslims were banned from discoveries or inventions.

5.4. Einstein's Relativity

On the dawn of the twentieth century, mankind stumbled on the newly found **subatomic phenomena** of x-ray, radioactivity, and subatomic particles. Theoreticians and experimentalists engaged in a century of digging, hypothesizing, and comparing between their ideas and realistic facts.

Like the birth of Islam which ignited a revolution of thoughts surrounding the nature of the creator and deterministic versus fatalistic scopes of human mind, scientific theories competed for deciphering new realities. Some **theories** gained the trust of scientists, others appealed more to laymen and fictionalists than to scientists.

The theory of relativity sanctioned the failure of experimentalists to detect the dependence of the speed of light on the speed of the source that emits it. Hence, **Albert Einstein** advanced the theory of special relativity on the premise that the speed of light was an absolute constant of nature.

Albert Einstein (1879-1955)   Ernest Rutherford (1871-1937)

Nobel Prize in Physics 2013 given on the discovery of **"God's Particle"** is also consistent with Nobel Committee's rejection of Einstein's claim that Aether could be avoided by relativity.

Even though Einstein is known with his famous statement "God does not play dice", yet Einstein did no more than playing dice by physics.
(1) **Albert Einstein** sweated in the two theories of relativity between 1905 and 1916, got the Nobel Prize 1922 for photoelectric effect, not relativity.
(2) **Max Planck** faced the same trouble, discovered the quantum 1900, awarded Nobel 1918.
(3) **Peter Higgs** proposed the Boson in 1964, got half Nobel Prize in 2013.
The three cases of Planck, Einstein, and Higgs show how the Nobel Committee drags its feet when it comes to theoretical physics.

In contrast to theoretical physics, **Ernest Rutherford** discovery of alpha-particles decay in 1899 awarded him the Nobel Prize ten years later. Rutherford latter discovered the nucleus, proton, neutron, and transmutation of element, which should have awarded him Nobel Prize on each of them.

Being from Newton's school of scientific integrity, Ernest Rutherford was the envy of German and French zealous rivals, was dismissed from any **American educational science books**. Instead Einstein's cigar and messy hair were used to glorify Einstein's secular transgression on God.

The British school of Newton and Rutherford proved that **God works in the lab**.

Liberal secularists squander their brains on hallucinatory theoretical physics, replaced Jesus Christ by Albert Einstein for the simplest reason of brain-washing young minds that eccentric and odd personal behaviors were conducive to genius **innovation and brilliance**.

Ernest Rutherford entered history as the father of nuclear physics.

On the dawn of the twentieth first century, NASA's folks started talking about "**Evicting Einstein**". NASA's house divided over our fundamental understanding of the universe based on Einstein's relativity and the "standard model" of quantum mechanics.

No one was able to reconcile the curved mass-filled spacetime of Einstein versus the flat particles-filled quantum spacetime.

Einstein's theory of relativity failed to explain essential facts proposed by Isaac Newton. According to Newton, if all the stars of the Milky Way travel at the speed of light, we will never know or feel the uniform motion. That explains why scientists never gave up on the idea that the constancy of the speed of light was questionable.

In addition, we cannot claim or prove that time is absolute in the remote universe. Even the atomic clock cannot be calibrated on a planet like Jupiter at $-100°$ C when Jupiter's year is about 11.86 Earth years.

We cannot prove that the rotation around the sun is an absolute unit of time in the far universe. In other words, in remote parts of the universe, time and distance might not be absolutes or even linearly proportional to ours, since we have never proved that time has an established universal constant unit.

5.5. Formidable and Divine

As stated above, the theory of evolution sat comfortably behind the castle of biological sciences shielded from the aggressive warring in physics and mathematics. **Darwin** refrained from the formidable challenge of origin of life despite entitling his work to allude to the contrary.

Similarly, **Isaac Newton** faced the exact problem when attempting to define the origin of force. Newton tackled the obvious behavior of matter when acted upon by force and was able to carve the most ingenious canons of matter and energy.

Newton summed the heavenly laws of the divine to justify that no matter could act without an actor, the action depends on the magnitude of force, and the universe must remain in equilibrium by resisting actions by reactions.

The nature of the **original actor** was abandoned by Newton, in the same manner that Darwin abandoned the creator or originator of the living matter.

The two dismissals by Darwin and Newton encouraged Einstein to attack Newton's absolute pillars of nature, the inertia (mass), space (length), and time (tempo). Einstein adopted very primitive geometrical rules to attribute the **relativity of time** to the speed of matter.

Not that the light speed, per se, entails space and time and thus cannot lead to breaching Newton's classical mechanics, but that **Einstein's theory of relativity** remained impotent for a century without any possibility to milk Einstein's cow beyond its philosophical transgression on classical mechanics.

Einstein's fantasies enticed many astronomers to indulge in greater fictional scientific undertakings such as the **Big Bang** and the age of the universe.

In parallel, evolutionists engaged in similar dating of species and planets, as if time was already known linear, constant, and reversible. Fantastic information was born anew. The age of earth four billion years, the **Big Bang** around 13 billion years, the life of species two million years, etc.

Those fantasies tainted modern science with fictional tales mostly designed to push religions into oblivion. Not by intention, but by **emptiness of boredom**.

In such frenzy of entangling fiction with facts, many teachers of science dismissed the stark fact that our perception is entirely hypothetical on matters such as the remote space, remote time, insides of planets or stars where our instruments cannot reach, and in the extremely minute subatomic space

We **cannot prove beyond doubt** that light travels at the same speed in the remote universe, as we cannot prove that time possesses any material features of linearity or constancy.

In the west, the theory of relativity was abandoned as the United States aimed at practical sciences that could generate revenues and advance economy. There was nothing good that relativity could offer beside science fiction movies and books that dispute the meaning of time.

Universities taught the **theory of relativity** in their schools of physics, which in turn lost credibility in graduating students with fictional sciences not suitable to practical applications.

In contrast to the alienation of the theory of relativity, the **theory of evolution** flooded every school, from elementary grades to college. Evolution books were rich in photographic display entangled with biochemical tales on the genetic origin of evolution.

5.6. Classical Statistics

Since time is the major pillar of **Newton's mechanics** that daunted researchers and posed absolute obstacles to scientists to probe remote space or decipher the mystery of origin of matter, energy, or life, compounded by the odd nature of time of forward growth without any possibility to reverse such growth, we doubt that time can be used to determine ages of planets, or species, or celestial entities.

We lack any criteria that could affirm or reject that a **century of time** in the present equals any similar period in the remote past or remote space. Also, since our sole time landmark is based on the earth-sun relationship, we cannot prove that the remote space recognized such time reference or standard or ages at our time rates.

The closest we could get to understand the odd nature of the constant growth of time and the inevitability of reversing such elusive pillar of nature lies in the **atomic system**. As all matter consist of atoms, and as the number of atoms comprising any material object was never determined definitely, as every subatomic particle was found to be composed of yet smaller entities, Boltzmann and Max Planck counted on the concept of **entropy** to describe basic quantum events in nature.

In Boltzmann's statistics, changes in heat or energy impose new atomic states amounting to **chaos**. The change in the atomic states due to changes in energy is measured as **temperature**. Hence, **entropy** or the ratio between change in energy and the temperature of the medium is the only physical phenomenon that mimics time.

Entropy never decreases because the very minute atomic entities can never resume their initial locations after getting agitated by change of energy.

Those subatomic events alone lend the time its **constant growth** and **impossibility of reversing** chaos to initial state.

Chaos evolves to new chaos which becomes the new equilibrium created by change in energy.

Entropy thus requires two essentials pillars of nature: **matter** and **energy**. There cannot be temperature change without material particles to deliver such sense of temperature. Similarly, there cannot be change of energy unless there are material entities to convey energy.

According to Planck, there exist a definitive universal constant, the **quantum** that determines the minimal change of energy that could create a unit change in state. For example, an amount of water heated by certain amount of heat will change from liquid state to vapor state depending of the change of entropy.

But, even if the change of heat was reversed in the exact amount, there is **no chance** that the atoms of vapor will return to the same locations of the initial atoms of liquid, even though the vapor condenses back to liquid. That should explain the close similarity between **time and entropy.**

Thus, if time can be attributed to behavior of matter due to **energy change**, one question how chaos and chance could evolve into the creation of life without mysterious effect imposed, either on energy or on matter or both. Whatever that effect turns to be, the intricacy of the human mind, the diversity of life on earth, and the **exclusivity of evolving life on earth** among the entire universe, make the concept of Divine inevitable.

5.7. Spirit and Matter

5.7.1. Limitations of material sciences

The split of modern sciences into physical and humanitarian branches and the short-winded mindset of creating **assembly-line education** system geared for producing job candidates, all led to a generation of literate people unaware of the significance of integrating physical and humanitarian sciences in enriching human qualities. The two polish the mind, soul, and body.

There is no doubt that understanding a scientific law, such as **Boyles Law** between pressure and volume of gas and mastering its applications enables man to deal with specific mechanical matters. However, managing the external world does little in dealing with the emotional nature of creatures.

Man's curiosity goes beyond understanding the laws of nature. Those are discovered by belated scientists. Even though man has inferred many governing laws of nature and realizes that many more laws remain to be discovered, the underlying forces behind those laws share the same features of the forces that drive our human mind.

As daunting and intriguing the greater universe to man's curiosity, yet the immediate work of every man's mind leads individuals to seek deeper insight into the **cause and purpose of life**. A young child could easily believe that people go to heaven after death. Then the child seeks greater details about the location of heaven and the means of going there. As those pursuits are blocked by physical impossibilities, the child would seek a real definition for life, birth, and forces behind those mysterious events.

As the child grows past the stage of concrete thinking, the child faces the limitations of the physical **scientific method**. This omits the reasons beyond the physical constants. Scientific methods merely formulate rigid laws that could predict similarly encountered events but do not delve into their genesis.

For example, Newton's law of universal gravitation was deduced from Kepler's three laws of planetary motions. Isaac Newton guessed that Kepler's observation on the motion of the earth around the sun must entail the **third pillar of nature** (masses of earth and sun) beside the two pillars given by Kepler (distances and time).

Hence, Newton suggested that the masses of the star and sun were the origin of gravity. That led to the **universal gravitational constant** $67384E-11$ N(m/kg)^2.

Prior to Newton, man's immediate logic was that there must be some **heavenly forces** that pull the planets to the sun or the moons to the planets. Yet, all that Newton could do was calculating the proportionality constant between the effect and the magnitude of masses of the celestial objects.

For a curious and inquisitive mind, such pragmatic approach to nature, by an observing Kepler and calculating Newton, affirms the **inevitability of the creator** behind our inferred universal constants. It is our admission that we can observe God's work, but we do not have the privilege of direct contact with the creator.

5.7.2. Limitations of spiritual sciences

Mental forces shared by all human minds entail many recognizable constants and laws in the same fashion encountered in the universal physical constants and laws. All animal species exhibit characteristic patterns of mental development and growth landmarks.

Among those shared mental constants and laws are shared **mood**, shared **intellect**, and shared **behavior** of human beings along the life-curve of development and growth. Humans develop through well-predicted **mental and physical landmarks** through life. Those made possible the establishment of civilized human communities.

Those who deviate severely or moderately from those landmarks, on the low or the high ends, comprise either burden on the community or its stars, leaders, and geniuses.

Therefore, **heavenly canons of faith befit heavenly creatures**, with heavenly conferred minds.

We cannot claim that the pattern of mental constants and laws were not heavenly since no physical agency could generate similar designs.

Those canons inspired by religious messengers guide those mental effects such that man settles on defined boundaries in human interactions.

In the barren desert of the Arabian peninsula of the seventh century, Prophet Muhammad journeyed south in winter, north in summer, met merchants from Asia and Africa in the south, from Europe and north Asia in the north. Islam was born on that world bridge between the **minds of diverse cultures** of Asia and Europe.

The **bridge of minds** is formed form memorized and vocalized Quran. Its ideas and sounds transcend man's cumulative memory along successive generations of men. Memories of colorful universe, the creator sets canons of conducts, rewards and retributions, through mental censors not physical actors.

Even in the most secular cultures that reject the personalized image of God of **Trinity** of son, father, and holy ghost, people still show love to creatures such as pets, plants, and others fulfilling and enriching natural entities. The mindset of appreciating creatures as long as they carry no connotation to religious ideas shows that some people are fed up with the rigid depiction of God in a matter in which Church alone likes people to believe.

What follows after adopting the Church's favored concept of Trinity enforces the concept of utilizing religion to control others. In **John 14:6**, the Bible states:

"I am the way, and the truth, and the life; no one comes to the Father but through Me."

Even though Prophet Muhammad is described in Quran as the messenger of mankind, Muhammad established Quran over twenty years, led armies to wars, lived and died in the process of establishing a new religion that changed the course of history, yet without invoking intangible magical miracles.

Muhammad's immediate associates carried over Islam to remote cultures. Thus, Muhammad's deeds, not his ego or preferred status, sufficed convince the followers of Islam that Muhammad was not only human like them, but was also an illiterate, sheep herder, and poor Bedouin.

Neither was Muhammad a noble man, nor was he wealthy, nor did Muhammad asked people to do what he could not do.

Being poor and earthly, Muhammad appealed to the sweeping majority of people throughout the history of Islam. The few wealthy people were also compelled to believe Muhammad because wealthy people cannot survive without the poor labor of all communities.

Regardless of the score of **sporting religions**, personal conviction is mostly subjective, illogical, and ingrained and anchored at young age. Therefore, the validity of religious canons matters less on the personal conviction.

That is not so on global, societal, or herd conviction. Clearly, in the west, Christianity receded to the poor and moderately educated classes and nations. Higher classes adopt religious rituals as formalities or as clout for faith regardless of the inconsistencies in religion.

In the west, Mormonism succeeded in building stronger family ties and produced highly disciplined Christians despite the irrationality of Joseph Smith and his bizarre claims that he was handed **golden plates** by a holy ghost. Those were translated to the **Book of Mormon.**

The Mormon Church in Salt Lake City, Utah, dedicate three levels of rooms to its followers, each level depends on the monetary contribution of the follower. The highest paying follower is promised access the holiest room, where the follower could be heard straight by God. Such short-sighted logic might enrich the Church on expedient bases, but it repulses greater segments of people that cannot sanction illogical beliefs.

CHAPTER 6

The Fight For Egypt

6.1. Population Explosion versus Depletion of Resources

Mohamed Hosni Mubarak ruled Egypt between 1981 and 2011. The Egyptian population increased from 44.9 million in 1980 to 84.0 million in 2011.

As Mubarak aged, spent thirty years chasing his rivals out of power, Mubarak developed unshakable delusion of the ultimate Pharaoh.

The doubling of human population and freezing of economic and social development filled the Egyptian streets with homeless and desperate people, the roads with the most luxurious cars, and the sea shores with the most lavish mansions and places.

Neighboring Egypt, all Arab states suffered from the same problems of population explosion and unequal distribution of wealth. Millions of Egyptians working in the oil-rich nations were compelled to return home from Libya, Algeria, Saudi Arabia, Iraq, and the gulf-states.

During the 1991's Iraq-Kuwait war, Saddam Hussein sent home thousands of coffins of Egyptians shot in the head because Egypt fought on the side of Kuwait.

6.2. Resisting Americanization

Emigration of Egyptians to Europe or to the Americas meant total **annihilation of the Islamic fiber** of families. Only Egyptian Copts viewed emigration to the west advantageous. Muslims incur greatest losses in the Christian west, where drugs, sex, and secular education are all the children could aspire for career-based education.

The western child is deprived from praying or religious education in public schools, but not prohibited from improvising fiction, acting, singing, or any field that is not related to the Bible or **morality or the Divine**.

Western children are nurtured to seek **empirical evidence**, denied equal depth in humanitarian sciences that deal with the mind, behavior, or mood. Mathematics and sciences scored high on all educational curricula.

The moral decay in American society crept insidiously into the Egyptian society as some liberals view the American liberalism an ideal option of **pragmatism and free thinking**.

The ancient tradition of **arranged marriages** or parents engaging in marrying their children, based on family reputation and personal integrity, is being questioned against the free choices given to American children.

Thus, at the **young age** when the child could easily make serious errors that affect his or her entire life, American children are insulated from the cumulative wisdom of old generations, mainly influenced by peer pressure and media marketing.

In addition to those burdens of liberal moral decay, which result in greater divorces and children left to the challenges of nurturing and education, muslims are confronted with greater challenges of **corruption and tyranny**. Those divert national resources to the pockets of the few.

As muslims find **western cultures** unfit to nurture their children on sound moral or humanitarian values, it behooves muslims to rectify the wrongs in their countries, so as to rear their children according the values they believe in.

Similarly, many American Jews view Israel a favorite milieu for rearing Jewish children away from the artificial secular exclusion of faith from public education. Those Jews suffered enormously on the hands of Christians in Russia, Europe, and the United States, **returned to Palestine to change its identity**, cleanse it from non-Jews, and build their own nest amidst hostile Islamic and Christian neighbors.

During the height of the second Palestinian intifada of 2003, Rachel **Aliene Corrie**, a 24 year old woman from Washington State of the United States was crushed to death on March 16, 2003 by an Israel Defense Forces armored bulldozer in Rafah, in the southern part of the Gaza Strip.

Egypt, in particular, possesses the unique condensation of population around the narrow strip of the River Nile, in addition to the **low mobility** of inhabitants far from their birth places. Such geographic makeup reduced the scattering of members of same families across the 25 providences of Egypt, either due to job opportunities or cost of living.

Like the west, **teaching Islam** in Egyptian schools raises the objection of Christians and makes the curriculum too ambiguous to achieve intended results. Despite those difficulties, both Islam and Christianity are taught in public schools, each religion taught to its student followers. Thus,

120

muslim students study Islam, Christian students Christianity. This differs from the purpose intended in teaching religions in the United States.

However, a great source of religious teaching in Egypt comes from **mosques** found in every street in every town or village in Egypt. In the same manner, many modern high rises in urban America dedicate a floor for gymnasium, Egyptian high rises often dedicate a room or basement for a mosque. That is beside the fully independent mosques in same neighborhoods.

Those freely accessible resources to Islamic teachings afford youth wide choices of views on Islam. In wealthier families, children are taught by **private tutors** at home. Many families could easily hire five or more tutors in various subjects, including Islam, in order to expand the knowledge of their children to the most. Many families commute their children to two or more sports training per week to fulfill the ancient dream of integrated body-mind-spirit.

6.3. Militarization of Society

6.3.1. Military Charisma

Dwight D. Eisenhower   Charles De Gaulle   Gamal Abdel Nasser

In the USA, Eisenhower's presidency was secured on the background of the man's advanced experience in WWII, the greatest war in history of mankind. In France, De Gaulle also acquired his experience in the same conflict. Both Eisenhower (president from 1953 until 1961.) and De Gaulle (president from 1959 until 1969) were born in 1890, arrived to power over the **age of sixty**.

In Egypt, Gamal Abdul Nasser was born 1918, arrived to power at the age of 34.

Nasser was seventeen years younger than General **Mohamed Naguib**, yet Nasser was seasoned in the extreme poverty and oppression in the remains of the Ottoman Empires. From start to end, Nasser completed his mission at the age of 52. Ten million people walked in his funeral. Those imprisoned by him praised him more than those prospered by his deeds.

121

Mubarak, 80 y   Nasser, 50 y   El-Sissi, 56 y

The gift of charisma plays into the fate of nations.

In 1968, **Gamal Abdul Nasser** was in his 50. He proved to be a phenomenal leader who chose to change history by ingrained Quranic nurturing, that God alone is the supreme creator. Nasser's teaching position in the Egyptian Military Academies and his upbringing in poor muslim family, (in Bakous, Alexandria, Egypt) contained the ingredients of new Islamic revolution.

The district of **Bakous** never ceases celebrating Islamic teachings in mosques, street gatherings, funerals, and underground meeting plotting to fight the British occupation and rectify the corruption of King Farouk.

The persona of a **historic leader** was embodied in Nasser's body motion, facial expressions, sound of vocalization of Arabic words, instantaneous humor, conforming to Islamic canons, and his military discipline.

6.3.2. Making A Tyrant

In 2011, **Hosni Mubarak** was 83, governed Egypt over 30 years. When millions of Egyptians waited in Tahrir Square to hear his resignation speech, Mubarak thought he could still sell his tired lies, promised to punish those who did wrong, promised to keep his words, **promised to work harder**.

Mubarak did the unthinkable as he said: **"Your killed and injured ones will not go in vain."**

Somehow, Mubarak forgot that those killed and injured civilians were his own people, killed by his orders in the **Battle of Camels**. Mubarak instructed his agents to gather bullies for hire,

122

ordered them to marsh on camels, donkeys, and whatever they could get, to attack the gathering of civilians in Tahrir Square.

In the **Battle of Camels**, February 2, 2011, Hosni Mubarak got help from the billionaires of the National Party. The billionaires used homeless men from the ghettos of Cairo and Giza, and all owners of camels, donkeys, and horses to disperse the rallies in Tahrir Square. The mob came to beat, kill, or chase civilian campers out of the square.

This was the **turning point** in Mubarak's removal on February 11, 2011.

This poor camel owners or leasers were handed a job to kill, beat, or chase people opposing Hosni Mubarak.

This young man never expected to act in a real life movie. He was paid to ride his horse, use the steel bar to hit, kill, and chase people.

This is not theatrical acting. Those are camels and horses belonging to the people living around the Pyramids of Giza, Cairo. Those people were hired by Mubarak's aides to disperse the crowds of civilians seeking change of Mubarak's brutal regime.

The Battle of Camels included donkeys and horses beside camels. There are about 300,000 homeless people hired by the Egyptian police for looting and apprehending civilians without identification papers or uniform. All secret police in Egypt are not in uniform and could commit serious crimes. Those are attached falsely to Islamists in order to get indictments against them.

Trained camels are part of combat operation. This camel knows who to hit. His rider is a secret policeman holding a steel bar to kill, injure, and chase people out of the gathering rally.

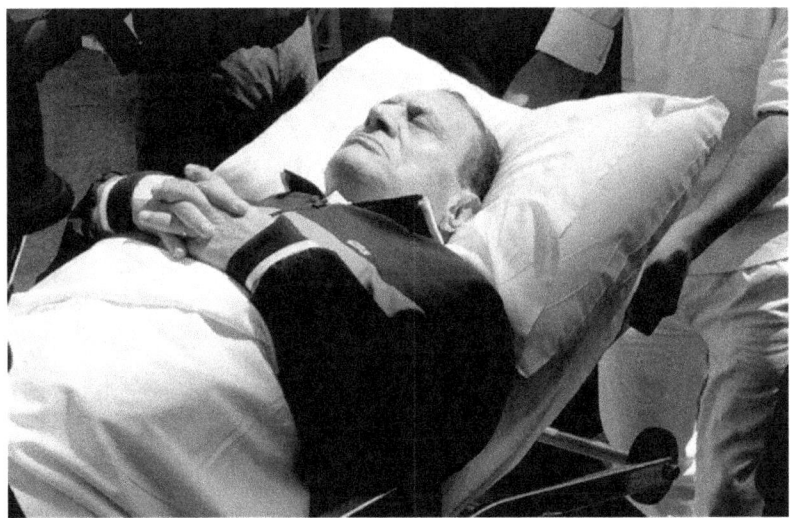

Mubarak played the bed-ridden elderly patient soon after he was forced to leave office. Until the last day of his presidency, Mubarak asked to be allowed to stay nine more months in order to allow for transition to the new president. After 30 years in power, public uproar left Mubarak no chance to fool around any longer. Mubarak resorted to the bed throughout all public appearances after his ousting. The shock of **losing eternity and glory** beyond man's limited life left Mubarak to such comical show of detached leader.

After retrial and sensing the pending coup against Mohamed Morsi, Mubarak sat instead of laying down. Gamal appears more confident and smiles for the first time in his life.

To Mubarak's credit, he was the only Arab tyrant arrested, tried, and imprisoned by the people he governed. In any other country, Mubarak and his family would have been shot dead by the millions who lost all livelihoods by Mubarak's crimes.

Mubarak was too dumb to sense the grave destruction of a nation by his selfishness and constricted intellect. Heikal told a story of a fellow who met with Mubarak, teased him about the glorious feeling of being the Pharaoh of Egypt sitting in the seat of president. Mubarak responded: "You could take my seat if you wish."

Mubarak's sons, Gamal (with elbow behind hid dad's head) and Alaa (turning his head to the jailer) were accused by **Mustafa El-Fiqi**, the Secretary of Mubarak from 1985 to 1992, as the reason for Mubarak's failure. El-Fiqi joked: "Mubarak let Gamal drive his car; Gamal slammed the car into a concrete wall." El-Fiqi is well-known with his street humor and ingenious ability to live around crooks and despots, changing his skin to adapt to whatever surround him.

El-Fiqi made the same ridiculous judgment when Erdogan begged Mubarak to leave office after 30 years of tyrannical ruling. Fiqi described Erdogan as the unfaithful friend who betrayed his old friend Mubarak. Somehow, El-Fiqi could not grasp the horror created by a military officer ruling Egypt for 30 years.

Mubarak's plan for passing presidency to his son Gamal Mubarak (on his right, left of reader) was spoiled by Mubarak's himself. Mubarak stated to Suzanne, his wife, that if he let Gamal take over publically, he would sit down do nothing in his old age. Mubarak feared that the military would reject the son of an ex-president who never wore the uniform.

Farther, Gamal Mubarak was dry, rigid, aloof, and entirely removed from people. Gamal was forced to hook with a woman after his mother complained of his inability to pick the right wife.

In contrast, Suzanne succeeded in picking an Egyptian beauty to **Alaa Mubarak** (right of reader), her younger son. Alaa Mubarak got married, had a son, which the grandfather Hosni Mubarak adored beyond anything in life. At the age of 13, Mohamed Alaa Mubarak, the grandson of Mubarak died in 2009, leading to the first tragedy in Mubarak's career and the one that paved the way for his docile approach to crushing his own people without mercy.

Gamal Mubarak (left) and Hosni Mubarak (right), both ended behind bars due to their lack of sensitivity to the disastrous economic crises they brought on Egypt for thirty years.

Hosni Mubarak remained vague on the issue of passing presidency to his son Gamal. Gamal adopted the western style of repeated polls to test his appeal for presidency. His total lack of public charm, charisma, or feeling of street men, entrapped him in prison. Mustafa Al-Fiqi described Mubarak's ambiguous stance of his son's future by saying:

"I listen to your promises I believe. I see your actions, I wonder."

Gamal Sadat (left), Anwar Sadat (right), Sadat named his son after his boss, President Gamal Abdul Nasser. The tradition of military officers naming their children after the president was joked at by Gamal Abdul Nasser. Nasser told Gamal Al-Sadat:

"You are hypocrite like your father."

Gamal Anwar Al-Sadat was luckier than Gamal Hosni Mubarak. Sadat was assassinated in 1981 before his son could have been corrupted by the supporters of Sadat. Those same supporters led Hosni Mubarak to plundering Egypt after the death of Sadat.

Gamal Sadat and his mother **Jihan Sadat** were great distinction from Nasser's family. The latter lived and died to serve Egypt and leave as poor as the rest of Egyptians. Sadat was the first president to promise Egyptians that corruption would be the norm and that if they cannot get rich in his time, they will never do under any other regime.

Both Mubarak's sons in prison suits. The white suit means that the prison inmate is innocent until proven guilty. Gamal Mubarak (named after Gamal Abdul Nasser) by his father Hosni Mubarak, who was promoted by Nasser to head Egypt's Air Force. The tradition of military officers naming their children after the president was a sure sign of obedience.

Gamal holds the Quran on the outside of court papers, in a naïve and comical gesture that would infuriate most muslims. The man who violated all essence of Quran is now seeking its mercy. Immediately, comedian Mohamed Fawzy Bakous joked that Gamal held the Quran during Morsi's rule, dropped it after El-Sissi ousted Morsi.

Gamal (left) and Alaa Mubarak (right) were nurtured and raised in a culture that would turn any child into a tyrant regardless of his race, country, or religion. Suzanne Mubarak was half-British, half-Egyptian, married Hosni Mubarak for his sexy military uniform and status. Hosni Mubarak was among the poorest Egyptian, who could not afford to leave military base or afford civilian cloth beside the military suits.

The mix of a wife remotely related to Quran and genuine Islamic upbringing and a father lacking any intellectual accomplishments beside the rigid military life-style, both led Mubarak, Suzanne, and the sons face the grave end of imprisonment and vast destruction of Egypt.

6.3.3. Military Coup

General **Sami Anan** served the despised, removed president Mubarak. Anan complained that general El-Sissi impeded his efforts to run for presidency. Like most Egyptian military officers, Anan relies on the models of general Eisenhower in the USA and general Charles de Gaulle in France to justify his competence to rule a nation.

Since the destruction and bleeding of Egypt were vividly protested on the streets, Heikal, the **philosopher of the ousting of Mubarak and Morsi**, advised the military establishment to hand the presidency to the political party with greatest resources. That is the Muslim Brotherhood.

Hence, rumors spread that the military establishment fixed up the election votes to make General **Ahmed Shafik** lose, and Morsi win. After sixty years of destruction of Egypt by three military presidents, Anan faced the upheaval of massive resentment to runners with military background.

In the background of the Egyptian chaos caused by the 2013's military coup, the Syrian revolution showed the **ruthless killing** for two years of civilians by their own government. That was preceded by similar blood-shed in Libya.

The uncanny realization of **Zawahiri and Sayyid Imam**'s prediction of formidable chaos, resulting from deviation from heavenly justice, lent islamists greater credibility. Not as realistic or objective alternative to secular democracy, but as the only alternative to thuggish plundering of the nation. The few military rulers lacked any conscience or feeling for the injustice inflicted on the impoverished majority.

In the foreground, the prominent military leader El-Sissi and all those supported him belong to the same defunct regime of Mubarak. Those were mostly **security, police, and military officers** deemed corrupt and rejected by Egyptians.

The historic moment of ousting Mohamed Morsi, on July on July 3, 2013, by Fattah El-Sissi shocked the world. In the most reckless move in the history of Egypt, the elected Egyptian president was arrested, locked up, and later charged by fabricated charges by his own minister of defense.

In the beginning El-Sissi struggled with speaking in public, could not pronounce full words, before he gained his composure. Since this speech was written by some literate writers, the speaker focused on the delivery of speech.

All plotted propaganda will fail to conceal the unfortunate stupidity of hijacking democracy by military officers. Scandals will erupt one after the other, thousands of lives will be lost, state emergency enacted, vice president ElBaradie resigns, the United States suspends military assistance, and El-Sissi seeks **immunity from persecution** in order to give up the military uniform.

In 2013, **Abdul Fattah El-Sissi** was 56, ousted Mohamed Morsi on the ground that many people flooded the streets seeking Morsi's removal. El-Sissi arrested Morsi and Islamists, imprisoned them and closed all Islamic TV stations.

The legal consequences of illegal coup permeated through the sentences. Never again did El-Sissi overcome the perception of his people and the world that he chose a route leading to his removal by death or imprisonment.

In his speech on October 6, 2013, El-Sissi could not deliver sentences before long pauses, deviating from script, and inserting slang sentences that caused ridicule, such as:
(1) "You are the pupil of our eyes"
(2) "Our hands will be cut if they extend to harm to our people."
(3) "The Great Prophet said you are the best sons on earth."
(4) "I swear on Allah the great, I swear on Allah the great, that is true, and you must believe me."

On the far left sat **Mohammad ElBaradie**, the Nobel Prize winner in peace. ElBaradie was criticized by millions of Egyptians, the prime minister of Turkey, and by many people who threatened him to withdraw the Nobel Prize from him for supporting the coup.

ElBaradie did not last long and fled to Austria after the massacre of Rabaa Al-Adawiya.

On the right sat **Ahmed Tayyib** the mofti of Azhar and **Pope Tawadros** of the Coptic Church, both would face enormous rejection as the blood bath got bloodier.

Few weeks after the military coup, El-Sissi started leaking more lies. Those were soon refuted by eyewitnesses.

He claimed that Morsi mixed cards by using religion in government, alienated judges, opposition, journalists, and military and therefore, he was compelled to listen to the public outcry to save Egypt from chaos.

The coup then entered Egypt into greater chaos, with intensified guerilla war in Sinai, massive riots and blood shed allover Egypt, and world shock from the uniformed military general in dark sun glasses, reminiscence of the Qaddafi, Saddam, Bashar Assad, and Manuel Noriega.

El-Sissi took great care in his military uniform to extent of his constant and frequent change of combat fatigue, to ceremonial uniform, decorated with flamboyant badges. While El-Sissi never participated in any combat operations, his first infamous mission was killing his own people.

Ironically, **General Manuel Noriega** of Panama, a nation with the same geographic importance of Egypt with its canal comprising a main water passage between the Atlantic and Pacific oceans, followed the same path upon which El-Sissi embarked.

Noriega strengthened his position as de facto ruler of Panama in 1983 by promoting himself to full general paid by the CIA. Noriega's poor understanding of world politics led him into conflict with the American government, which later ordered the invasion of Panama, the arrest of Noriega. He was tried, convicted, and sentenced to life in prison in the USA.

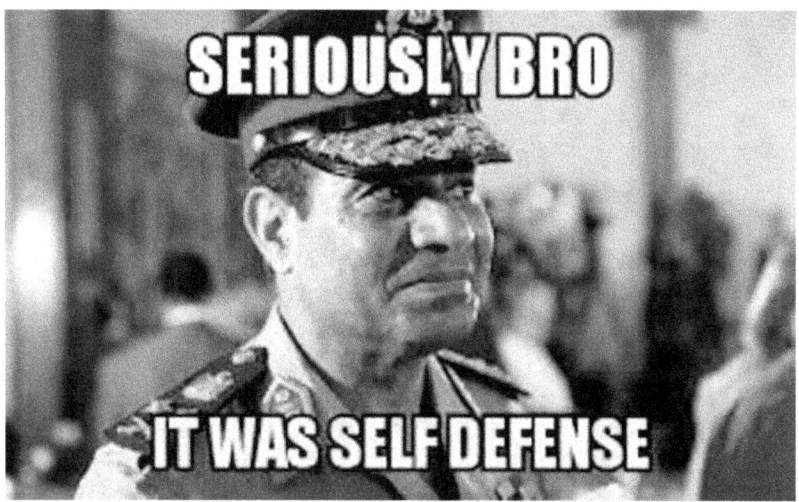

The massacre of Rabaa Al-Adawiya was the gravest landmark in El-Sissi's career.

To this date, October 11, 2013, General Abdul Fattah El-Sissi (sitting) and Interior Minister **Mohamed Ibrahim** (standing), the two plotted and executed many massacres tolling six thousands dead.

First suicide attempt to kill Ibrahim, in the middle of Cairo, failed. Yet all media news in Egypt do not cease warning the two of the inevitable pending attacks on their lives after committing unprecedented massacres and committed the capital crime of a military coup against democratically elected president.

Even though Mubarak escaped killing in 1981 and 1995, he lived 30 years with impeccable security measures and state-wide emergency law. But, the tide of history changed for ever. Killing and explosions are ongoing in every part of Egypt until El-Sissi and Ibrahim are brought to justice.

This ugly scene was unthinkable in the history of Egypt where people learned how to build peaceful and harmonious communities around the banks of the Nile. Rumors of jailed officers who refused to execute military orders to fight on the streets of their own country have not been substantiated. These poor soldiers will return to families that live under the line of poverty without the slightest hope to support the young, sick, or elderly, or even themselves. A lurking danger that could as well turn the military against its top leaders.

That military armored truck was purchased by the Egyptian people or given by the USA as collaterals to services. It is now roaming all Egyptian cities and high ways to contain civilian riots against the military coup.

Not that all American military assistance and warfare given to the Egyptian government since 1977 could not deter the civilian unrest and anger against the government, but that those soldiers are ordered to fire and kill civilians, own brothers, sisters, parents, and neighbors. In addition, they face extreme marginalization, both by the government and by society.

The Egyptian soldiers are those millions of Egyptians who are denied basic education, basic housing, employments, and denied all hope in the any future. Those are the same soldiers who abandoned their posts when riots against Mubarak persevered until his ousting. As a result, all Egyptian prisons were abandoned and neighbors entered prisons to release the locked up prisoners.

Tahrir Square is blocked to pedestrians from all accesses on October 11, 2013, as islamists spare no occasion to reverse the coup.

Fridays are always weekly religious and gathering days that always bring the largest crowds, but any other occasion that could inflame people's minds are also used to the most.

6.3.4. The Official Arabic Declaration of The General Leadership of Armed Forces

نص بيان القيادة العامة للقوات المسلحة

آخر تحديث: الخميس، 4 يوليو/ تموز، 2013، 00:42 GMT

وفيما يلي نص بيان القوات المسلحة:

إن القوات المسلحة لم يكن في مقدورها أن تصم آذانها أو تغض بصرها عن حركة ونداء جماهير الشعب التي استدعت دورها الوطني وليس دورها السياسي على أن القوات المسلحة كانت هي بنفسها أول من أعلن ولا تزال وسوف تظل بعيدة عن العمل السياسي.

ولقد استشعرت القوات المسلحة ـ إنطلاقاً من رؤيتها الثاقبة ـ أن الشعب الذي يدعوها لنصرته لا يدعوها لسلطة أو حكم وإنما يدعوها للخدمة العامة والحماية الضرورية لمطالب ثورته. وتلك هي الرسالة التي تلقتها القوات المسلحة من كل حواضر مصر ومدنها وقراها وقد استوعبت بدورها هذه الدعوة وفهمت مقصدها وقدرت ضرورتها واقتربت من المشهد السياسي آملة وراغبة وملتزمة بكل حدود الواجب والمسئولية والأمانة.

لقد بذلت القوات المسلحة خلال الأشهر الماضية جهوداً مضنية بصورة مباشرة وغير مباشرة لاحتواء الموقف الداخلي وإجراء مصالحة وطنية بين كافة القوى السياسية بما فيها مؤسسة الرئاسة منذ شهر نوفمبر 2012 ، بدأت بالدعوة لحوار وطني استجابت له كل القوى السياسية الوطنية وقوبل بالرفض من مؤسسة الرئاسة في اللحظات الأخيرة، ثم تتابعت وتوالت الدعوات والمبادرات من ذلك الوقت وحتى تاريخه.

تلا السيسي البيان

كما تقدمت القوات المسلحة أكثر من مرة بعرض تقدير موقف إستراتيجي على المستوى الداخلي والخارجي تضمن أهم التحديات والمخاطر التي تواجه الوطن على المستوى الأمني والاقتصادي والسياسي والاجتماعي ورؤية القوات المسلحة كمؤسسة وطنية لاحتواء أسباب الانقسام المجتمعي وإزالة أسباب الاحتقان ومجابهة التحديات والمخاطر للخروج من الأزمة الراهنة.

فى إطار متابعة الأزمة الحالية اجتمعت القيادة العامة للقوات المسلحة بالسيد رئيس الجمهورية فى قصر القبة يوم 22 يونيو 2013 حيث عرضت رأي القيادة العامة ورفضها للإساءة لمؤسسات الدولة الوطنية والدينية، كما أكدت رفضها لترويع وتهديد جموع الشعب المصري.

ولقد كان الأمل معقوداً على وفاق وطني يضع خارطة مستقبل ويوفر أسباب الثقة والطمأنينة والاستقرار لهذا الشعب بما يحقق طموحه ورجاءه ، إلا أن خطاب السيد الرئيس ليلة أمس وقبل إنتهاء مهلة الـ 48 ساعة جاء بما لا يلبي ويتوافق مع مطالب جموع الشعب، الأمر الذي استوجب من القوات المسلحة استناداً على مسئوليتها الوطنية والتاريخية التشاور مع بعض رموز القوى الوطنية والسياسية والشباب ودون استبعاد أو إقصاء لأحد، حيث اتفق المجتمعون على خارطة مستقبل تتضمن خطوات أولية تحقق بناء مجتمع مصري قوي ومتماسك لا يقصي أحداً من أبنائه وتياراته وينهى حالة الصراع والانقسام. وتشتمل هذه الخارطة على الآتي :

تعطيل العمل بالدستور بشكل مؤقت .

يؤدى رئيس المحكمة الدستورية العليا اليمين أمام الجمعية العامة للمحكمة .

إجراء انتخابات رئاسية مبكرة على أن يتولى رئيس المحكمة الدستورية العليا إدارة شئون البلاد خلال المرحلة الانتقالية لحين إنتخاب رئيس جديد.

لرئيس المحكمة الدستورية العليا سلطة إصدار إعلانات دستورية خلال المرحلة الانتقالية.

تشكيل حكومة كفاءات وطنية قوية وقادرة تتمتع بجميع الصلاحيات لإدارة المرحلة الحالية.

تشكيل لجنة تضم كافة الأطياف والخبرات لمراجعة التعديلات الدستورية المقترحة على الدستور الذي تم تعطيله مؤقتاً.

مناشدة المحكمة الدستورية العليا لسرعة إقرار مشروع قانون انتخابات مجلس النواب والبدء في إجراءات الإعداد للانتخابات البرلمانية.

وضع ميثاق شرف إعلامي يكفل حرية الإعلام ويحقق القواعد المهنية والمصداقية والحيدة وإعلاء المصلحة العليا للوطن.

اتخاذ الإجراءات التنفيذية لتمكين ودمج الشباب في مؤسسات الدولة ليكون شريكاً في القرار كمساعدين للوزراء والمحافظين ومواقع السلطة التنفيذية المختلفة.

تشكيل لجنة عليا للمصالحة الوطنية من شخصيات تتمتع بمصداقية وقبول لدى جميع النخب الوطنية وتمثل مختلف التوجهات.

تهيب القوات المسلحة بالشعب المصري العظيم بكافة أطيافه الالتزام بالمظاهر السلمي وتجنب العنف الذي يؤدي إلى مزيد من الاحتقان وإراقة دم الأبرياء. وتحذر من أنها ستتصدى بالتعاون مع رجال وزارة الداخلية بكل قوة وحسم ضد أي خروج عن السلمية طبقاً للقانون وذلك من منطلق مسئوليتها الوطنية والتاريخية.

كما توجه القوات المسلحة التحية والتقدير لرجال القوات المسلحة ورجال الشرطة والقضاء الشرفاء المخلصين على دورهم الوطني العظيم وتضحياتهم المستمرة للحفاظ على سلامة وأمن مصر وشعبها العظيم.

حفظ الله مصر وشعبها الأبي العظيم ... والسلام عليكم ورحمة الله وبركاته.

Out of power, all leaders of Muslim Brothers were rounded and sent to prisons, leaving the major national mess to the confused and shallow Abdul Fattah El-Sissi.

El-Sissi's total lack of skill in vocalizing Quran and total poverty of the contents of Quranic verses confronted the worst challenges in his life. He hid behind the façade of **Adly Mansour** and **Mohamed ElBaradie**. That latter bailed out of the government after the first massacre against **Rabaa El-Adawiya** that comprises the darkest event in the history of contemporary Egypt.

After few speeches by El-Sissi, Egypt was gripped by violence and riots due to El-Sissi' s embarrassing emptiness and lack of Islamic core values. The power of Islamic figurative treasures and the skills of vocalization inherited in every village in Islamic nations skipped the speech of General Abdul Fattah El-Sissi.

The most prominent and unforgettable statements that will haunt El-Sissi even after his death are the following:

السيسى: «تتقطع إيدينا قبل ما تتمد على واحد مصرى»

نشر فى : الأحد 28 أبريل 2013 - 11:36 م | آخر تحديث : الأحد 28 أبريل 2013 - 11:36 م

السيسى:"نروح نموت أحسن لو مقدرناش نحمى الشعب"..
ولن نسمح بدخول مصر فى نفق مظلم أو القتال أو الفتنة الطائفية

In the first, El-Sissi used an expression inappropriate for educated Arabs or Egyptian. El-Sissi stated:

"Our hands should be cut if they extend to reach an Egyptian"

Not that El-Sissi followed up by killing, burning, and imprisoning thousands of Egyptians, but that such swearing style imposes superstitious belief that higher power would cut the hands of those who do those acts.

Of course, El-Sissi went unpunished for the worst massacres committed by Egyptian governments against Egyptian people in Rabaa Adawiya.

In the second, El-Sissi adopted the same low level of reliance on Arabic or Quranic heritage by stating:

"We better go and die if we cannot protect the people and will not permit Egypt slip in dark tunnel or fighting or sectarian sedition."

The power of Quranic vocalization and vast figurative verses created an army of civilian youths empowered with the stern calling of Quran that the right path must be led by the faithful, not the devilish military officers.

The historic Islamic roots are strengthened by two major forces.

The high speed electronic communication and world travel of Egyptians.

Those exposed the close minds and futility of **militarism**. That is farther augmented by the historic failures of Arabs and Egyptian military in securing their people or caring for their own races.

Feast of Pilgrims (or Aid Al-Adha), October 14, 2013. Ramses Square, Cairo, Egypt.

The utter stupidity of the Egyptian military coup is such squandering of national treasures on every street in Egypt. During the extreme shortage of fuel, electricity, and food, those massive steel tank are destroying every remaining street pavement, their men are stranded in hot weather without access to public bathrooms or cold drinks.

The haunting of the criminals responsible for Rabaa Al-Adawiya and Nahda massacres and many other unforgotten deaths will not be deterred by the military show of power, since those soldiers belong to the murdered people.

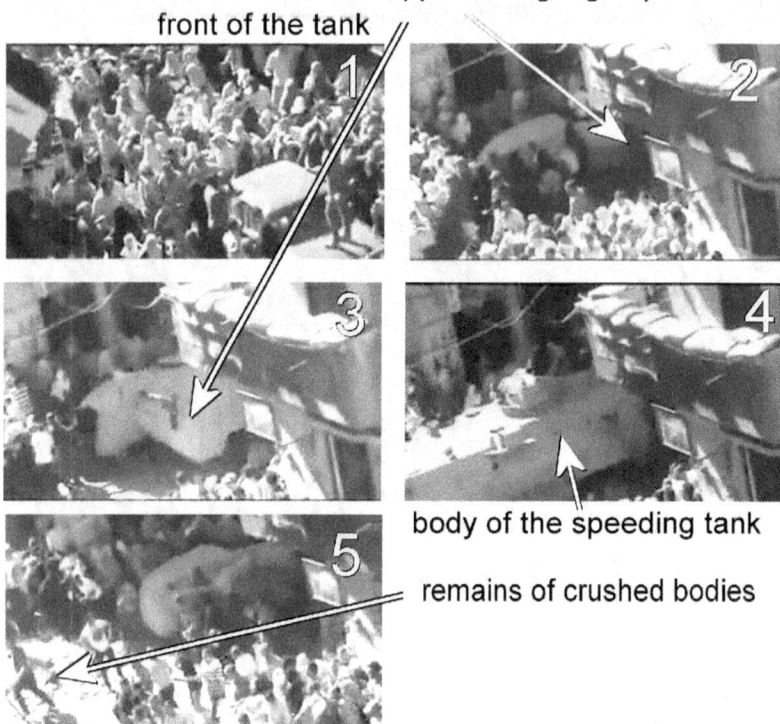

approaching high speed tank

front of the tank

body of the speeding tank

remains of crushed bodies

On October 11, 2013, those video clips of: (1) a tank running through a crowd rallying at night in the district of **Sidi Besher**, Alexandria, Egypt. (2) As the tank approached, few people alerted the crowd by loud speakers, (3) but the noisy crowd and the elderly participants did not give amble time to everyone to jump off the way of the tank. (5) Those crushed by the tank are left on the ground while the crowd still in shock of the horror scene.

Egypt's Army Spokesman Colonel **Ahmed Ali** became jocular cartoon for his inability to deliver smooth articulation of sentences, stressed with critical questions regarding the illegal behavior of military men and dragging the nation in such blood bath.

The wide gap between eloquent and purposeful Islamic speeches loaded with figurative verses from Quran and the dry, rigid, and empty words delivered by a shaking young officer is one among many factors that pushed El-Sissi on an inevitable path of destruction and despair.

El-Sissi recruited **Al-Arabiya** TV Channel to personify the speaker as young sexy male who captivate the hearts of female lovers and fans. This western style of marketing and alleviating humor fired back in a country confronted with daily gruesome deaths and destruction committed by the military coup.

CHAPTER 7

Rabaa Al-Adawiya Massacres

7.1. Rabaa Al-Adawiya alive

Before August 14, 2013, the square of Rabaa Al-Adawiya was the **Mecca of Muslim Brothers**, which produced greatest speeches, talents, ideas, and later, death and destruction.

Realizing that he is honored to fight for Islam, this father brought his toddler to the Mecca of Jihad in Rabaa Al-Adawiya. Soon, every one will have to fight for survival.

In the background, millions of Islamists and their supporters gathered in Rabaa Al-Adawiya Square, in Cairo Egypt from June 30, 2013 through August 14, 2013. Many of those campers were slaughtered on the August 14th massacres committed by the military and police through helicopters, bulldozers, armored vehicles, snipers, and proxy bullies.

The campers used sand bags and concrete blocks to impede military invasion.

Awaiting the return of mother, this sister took care of the baby of another lady, who would perish in the massacre. The baby is orphaned like millions of children in Egypt whose parents succumbed to the brutal injustice of corrupt governments.

Suzan Mubarak, the wife of the removed ex-president, hired experts to coach her on how to win Nobel Prize for peace by solving the problem of homeless children. The professor who helped Suzanne complained that her activities were robotics, aimed solely to gaining publicity, not to solve the roots of the escalating problem of homelessness. Suzanne blamed her husband for not transferring presidency to his son Gamal Mubarak earlier. Mubarak resisted transfer of power to his son explaining that he would sit down doing nothing if he gives up power.

They read the Quran.
They were told that the Quran can protect them against the mightiest evil on earth.
They might have died, lost.
But, the mission is intensified.
No mission triumphed without martyrs.
Their death was by deception.

7.2. Massacre Begins

The army and police did the unthinkable, used massive force to evacuate the two squares, Rabaa and Nahda, left the entire nation unprotected, which caused massacres, burning, and destruction in remote towns of Egypt.

The news of dead relatives in the two squares ignited waves of retaliation for the relatives of the dead people from the police. The deadly course of the military coup started.

As bulldozers ran over tents and people, the campers resisted by throwing whatever they could get on the police force. The campers realize that the police represents illegal military coup.

The bulldozers that were used to remove, crush, or run over civilians in Rabaa Al-Adawiya faced the two evils: either killing the unarmed civilians or getting killed by government snipers on roof tops and in tanks of military leaders.

The smoke, tear-gas, odors of blood and dead turned Rabaa Al-Adawiya into a graveyard.

The police security collecting the book of Quran, considered the most sacred book in Islam. Those simple soldiers are taking great care in making sure that the Quran is handled with dignity.

They might not be able to read the Quran, but their belief in it is unquestionable by herd tradition.

Extreme moments of anguish, death, and betrayal in the Rabaa Al-Adawiya Square.

Few blocks away from the center of burning and destruction, this severely injured person was lucky to have three people helping him find his way to a hospital.

At different site, the destruction and burning is less visible.

The young girl refuses to leave after losing her loved ones, but the police insist to clear the place of campers. The red buckets are water containers for drinking and bathing.

154

This photo irritates Egyptians as the police not only dresses in the infamous form of **foreign occupiers,** equipped with foreign equipments, but also because of English letters "**Police**" when most Egyptian do not read foreign languages, and many are illiterate.

This old woman was lucky to survive. Many old campers died in Rabaa Al-Adawiya.

There has never been a single photo that shows police use **water hoses** to disperse rioters. Here, the police are not threatened by the rioters, yet ordered to shoot. Many shot protesters were targeted by snipers from half a mile away.

This couple might be the luckiest people to get out alive form the massacre site. They carry all their belongings to head home and tell the true story of the gruesome killings.

If it was true that the campers were armed, those three soldiers would have never stood in line amid the rubbish, surrounded by dead, injured, trapped, and hidden campers in all directions.

7.3. Destruction

The sign shop:

"No To The Coup"

"Yes To Legitimacy"

The **burning of Rabaa Al-Adawiya** was a turning point in Egypt's history.

There were thousands of people killed by police since the January 25, 2011's revolution against Mubarak. But, Rabaa Al-Adawiya's massacre is committed by well-identified state-officials and after courts vindicated prior state-officials from similar murders. It was clear that Egypt is run by murderers and judicial system serving them.

The word is now to the people.

A scene from hell.

Whether this man is holding a gun or a stick, is not known. The gruesome scene of destruction makes it hard to believe that there still is an enemy to fight in the neighborhood.

7.3. Shock and Disbelief

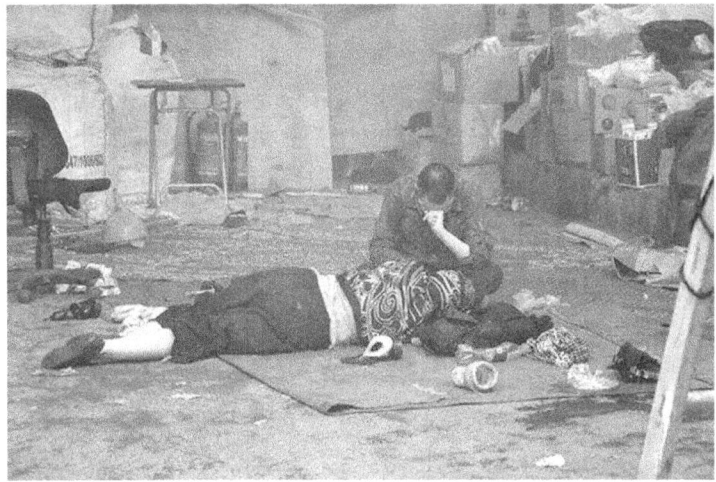

A man sitting at his wife place of death, few feet from where she was shot.

The infamous burning, destruction, and killings in the massacre of Rabaa Al-Adawiya.

The blockage of access to Rabaa Al-Adawiya on the dawn of August, 14 2013, shortly after 4:00 AM, Egyptian army and police moved on land and air to disperse thousands of civilian campers.

The police fabricated claims that it used water cannons before firing live-ammunition.

Their only chance for survival is burning fire.
The smoke reduced the effect of tear gases and reduced visibility for snipers.
The blaze impedes intruders.

The young man fallen behind the trash dumpster got a concerned woman calling for help.

Note, the woman appears anchored in the ground very close to the fallen man. Her concern for staying too close to fallen while calling for help speaks her empathy of a mother.

7.4. Rescue

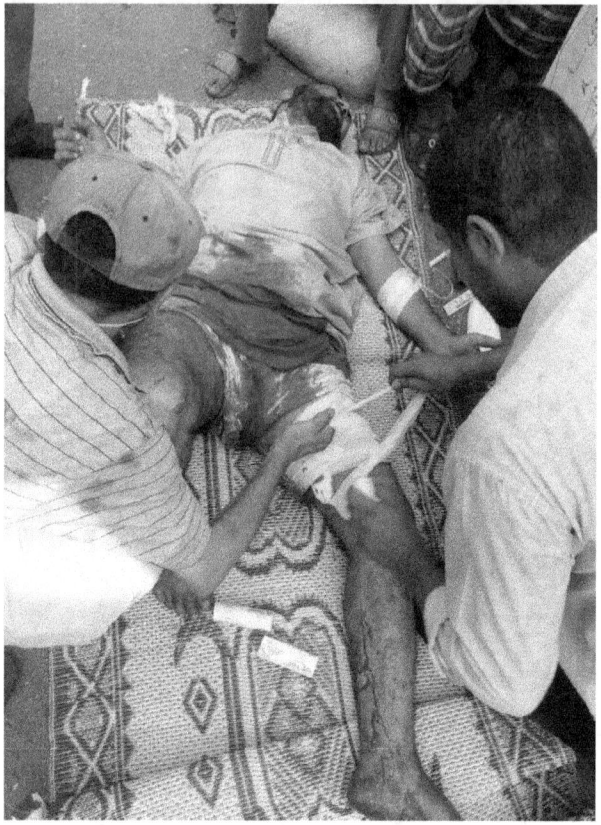

Field injury and wound caring on the carpet.
Notice the bare hands of the two men attending the care of the wounded.

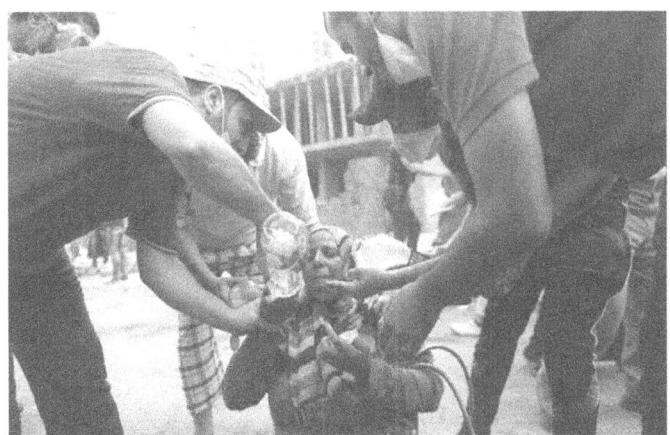

August 14, 2013, in the extreme heat of Egypt, those volunteers might be able to save that woman for now. But the road out of the square is filled with snipers and non-uniformed proxy muggers hired by many factions with diverse agendas.

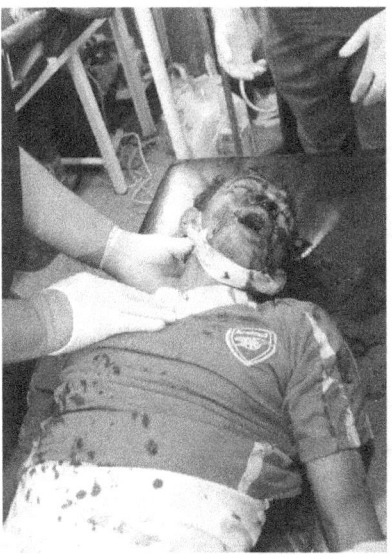

This unusual scene shows modern hospital equipments and proper care which is only available to police personnel. Injured civilians are cared for on the ground.

.

165

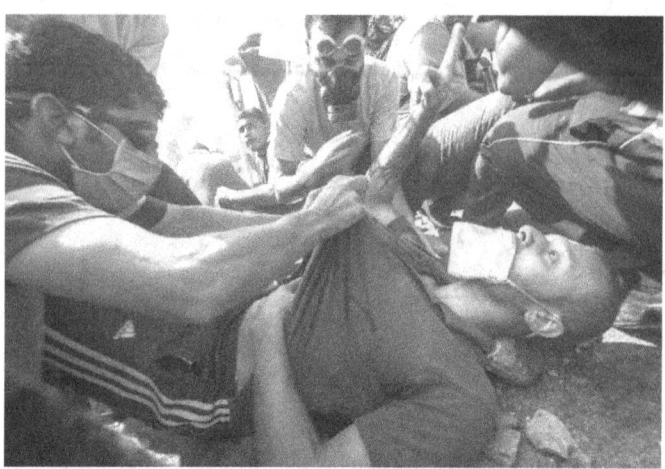

The index-up sign by the person laying on his back means: "**God is the only one greater than all**". It means that the person believes that if God wants him to live, God would send the agents, people and science, in the opportune time to save him. If he dies, then God wants him back. Or, that his fate is fairly determined.

The fallen soldier is always forgotten due to the side on which he fights, even though all those soldiers share same values of the people they fight. The few top officers who plotted for the massacre are seldom punished, either due to poorly funded and equipped general prosecutors or due to the vast authority that enables the state officials to conceal evidence of their crimes.

Three soldiers supervising the transfer of a fallen bearded citizen. No clues as to the status of that person.

It all bears the signs of chaos. The fire and smoke did not cause causalities as the deliberate and planned used of lethal weapons. Those were repeated in the January 25, 2011 by the same security secret police and their proxy army of non-uniformed bullies. For three years, claims of third party or foreign hands are suspected in cases of exploded skulls, chests, and guts by sniper bullets.

167

The grandmother might have been through hell many times in her life, but the young soldier appears in greater grief than the woman who lent him hand. Similar tragic incidents in the Egyptian history led to lingering plots of retaliation and terrorism by youth exposed to such unthinkable death toll.

Nothing this young man could do to comfort that woman who must have been through life-long tragedies of injustice, poverty, and despair, ended in such surreal scene of hell.

Bowing in owe in front of a grieving grandmother in the foreground of destruction is most probably an unconscious signature of empathy born out of mutual suffering.

7.5. Burning the mosque of Rabaa Al-Adawiya

This historic moment in the fight for Egypt's Islamic identity entails all elements that will carve the future of Islam.

Those civilians looking for loved ones will return to the twenty five providences of Egypt to face graver burning as the news are transmitted instantaneously by cell phones. Mostly, those six people in the scene of tragedy have less access to the greater tragedies than people sitting in front computer screens, hearing and seeing live uploads from different sites of massacres.

The Mosque of Rabaa Al-Adawiya, in Cairo, Egypt, on fire.

No drop of water was used in dispersing the campers of Rabaa Al-Adawiya despite the repeated speeches of Mohamed Ibrahim, the Interior Minister, claiming to have use water hoses to end the gathering peacefully.

Without burning tires, tents, clothes, and paper, the campers could be seen and shot by snipers from helicopters, armored vehicles, or from roof tops.

From afar, the streets of the camping ground of Rabaa Al-Adawiya are filled with smoke.

Mohamed Morsi's portrait stands tall amidst burning fire.

Hoping that smoke would reduce the effect of tear-gas canisters used to irritate eyes and lungs, or that smoke would impair visibility for snipers, or that fire might impede the advances of the police and army, the entire place was engulfed in fire set by many factions of different interests.

Concealing the numbers and identities of dead people was atop those government concerns. But, for islamists, the mosque turned into a grossly contaminated graveyard, the size of the crime exceeds all relief that could be gotten from forensic legal evidence.

It is a war, not a crime scene.

Amidst residential buildings, Rabaa Al-Adawiya turned into hell of death and destruction.

The charring remains of Rabaa Al-Adawiya are shown amidst crowded residential buildings.

As the dark sets on Rabaa Al-Adawiya on August 14, 2013, every thing was already burned.

The mosque of Rabaa Al-Adawiya was burnt by El-Sissi's troops on August 14, 2013. That was plotted by General **Fouad Allam,** as hinted by him on July 9, 2013 on Al-Arabiya TV, Al-Hadas program by Mahmoud Al-Warwary.

The disbelief that killing and burning a mosque in a muslim nation by muslim army and police was unthinkable to this young doctor, who might have never read on the history of state-committed massacres. He came here to save lives, but the army of his country wiped out thousands of families by its ignorance, impatience, and lack of realization of the grave consequences.

Inside the burnt mosque of Rabaa Al-Adawiya.

7.6. Unidentified dead bodies

The dead bodies inside Rabaa Al-Adawiya.

The left is declared "unknown".
The right is named "Abdul Nasser" from Qena, south Egypt.

فض اعتصام النهضة

A blanket was thrown on the body of young man whose brain is expelled outside his skull.

The photographer might have exposed the dead body in order to show this gruesome injury. The killed man was near Nahda Square near the University of Cairo, Egypt. The killed wore goggled to protect his eyes from tear gas. He was shot in the head.

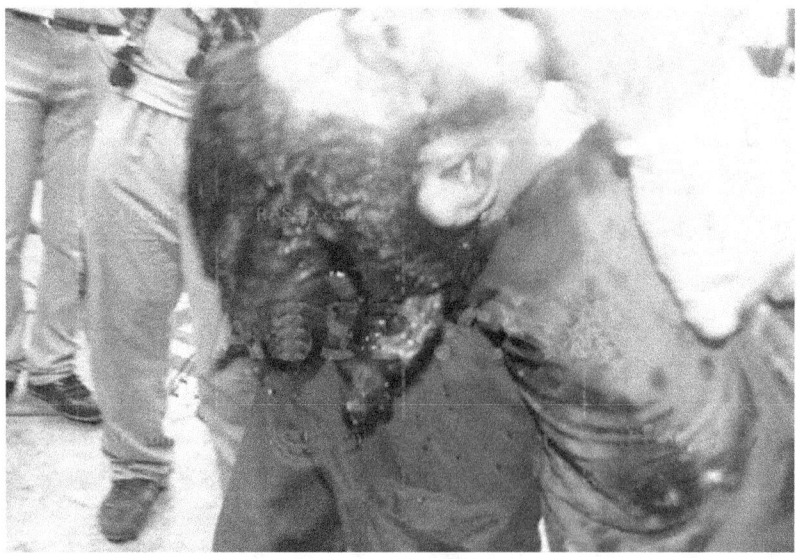

The introduction of cell phones and mobile cameras in the hands of almost everyone added this colorful tragedy to the story of state failure.

In the past, this gruesome scene of killing a civilian on the hands of police snipers were never seen or even perceived or believed.

On March 2013, Party leader **Abu Al-Ela Madi** accused the Egyptian General Intelligence establishment for organizing 300 thousand bullies behind the chaotic events in Egypt. The organization of bullies created by intelligence seven years ago then moved its supervision to the secret police. In Cairo alone, there are 80 thousand of those state-bullies.

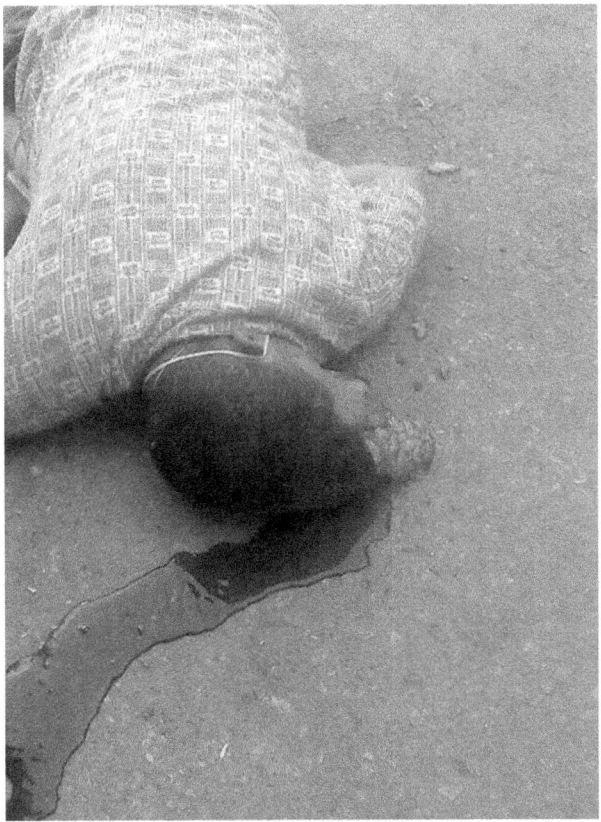

The white strip around the neck and ear are of tear-gas mask. This young man appears to have been shot from behind by explosive bullet that expelled his brain from his forehead. His blood is still pouring out fresh, shinning red, gushing in abundance.

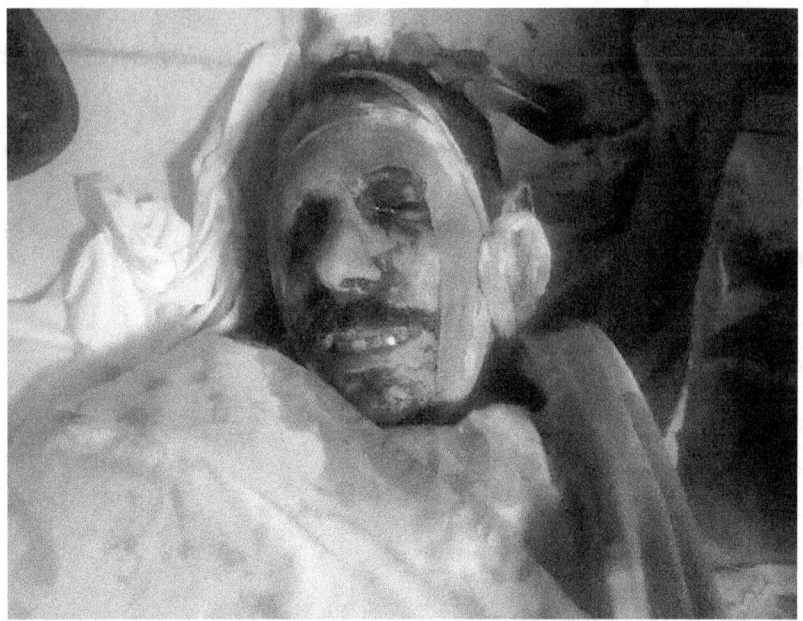

The symbol of misery, oppression, and suffering is magnified by the bloody death is the most honorable struggle for justice and inequality.

Neither the tear-gas mask nor the eye goggles spared this man's life from dying burned in Rabaa Al Adawiya.

From a distance, burning of tents over its inhabitants left the elderly and disable to perish. This man was charred to the extent that removing him would squander the time that could be invested to rescuing people who could live

Still finding dead and burned under the remains of Rabaa Al-Adawiya.

180

Searching for dead under blankets.

The person with the long stick does not cover his shoes and most probably does not wear gloves or mask. Those protective gears are in dire shortage as the state military and police is fighting those people seeking civilian government.

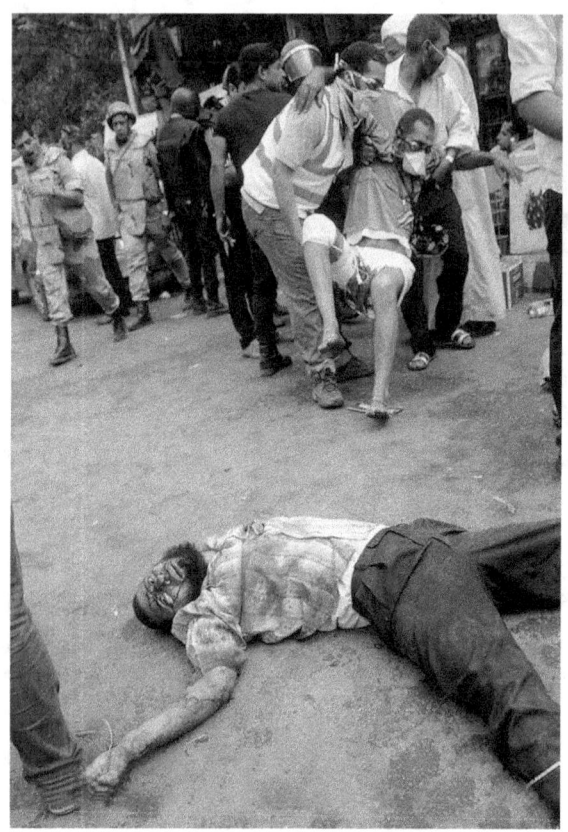

The dead is abandoned. The injured is rescued.

7.7. Protest

In English and Arabic, the sign shows that the Egyptians realize the unspoken fact that only foreign powers could impede the slaughtering campaign by the Army.

The Egyptian Army is equipped and funded by the USA since 1977. Before the USA replaced the British colonialist role after WWII, the English speaking white man has been the target of Muslim Brotherhood since 1928. The concept of **Hassan Al Banna**, in 1928, to revive the Islamic Caliphate, was the most viable and attractive ideology in the twentieth century. Then, Nazism was just brewing under the ashes. Communism was not yet put to test until the invasion of Poland by Hitler.

The
American armored vehicles are very new to the Egyptian streets and are used to commit massacres against unarmed civilian protesters by El-Sissi's military, after the total collapse of the interior ministry of police.

Also, very new on the Egyptian scene is this live video of an armored vehicle forced to jump off the bridge in order to avoid deadly attacks by rioters.

The police and army are now facing escalating anger from those who lost their relatives in government committed massacres.

This lightly armored van is used to disperse riots by tear-gas canister but could as well be attacked, captured, burned, and its occupants either escape or get killed.

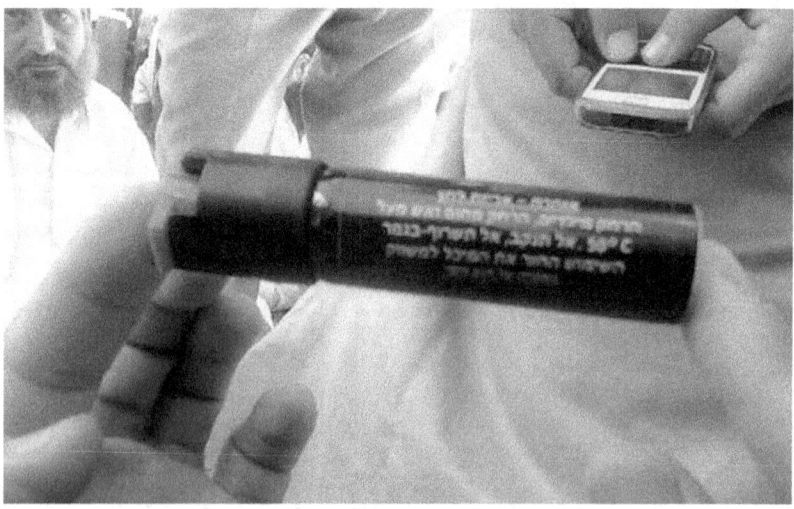

This tear-gas canister shows the Hebrew script and is shown to demonstrate the coordination of the Egyptian and Israeli effort to support the oppression of civilian protest. It is used to break riots and has caused direct injury on direct impact to the face or skin of rioters.

Rioters captured government armored vehicle and used it to celebrate their victory.

Many like those are arrested, tortured, and imprisoned. They may luckier than many killed rioters.

Few dozens arrested rioters were suffocated during transportation in police vehicles in August 2011, in Cairo, Egypt.

حرق مدرعات الجيش بالسويس

In the city of Suez on the Red Sea, this armored vehicle was hijacked and burned by rioters.

Fallen rioters have become common phenomena which have never been part of the Egyptian history, or was not seen prior to the era of cell phones and hand-held cameras.

188

In the hidden corners of the towns, the police recruit those civilian, homeless, or unemployed people, train them on police work, and used them to fight rioters. This is the only job that could bring money in those towns.

Morsi's photo posted high on the Statues of Cairo, Egypt. At the base, the graffiti reads:

"El-Sissi is the police dog.

The people want the execution of El-Sissi".

189

Military armored vehicles enforcing the emergency law and curfew at major cross roads.

7.8. Martyrs of Islam

Six thousand civilian Egyptians have been slaughtered by their own police and army, among 90 million people (impoverished by illiteracy, corrupt education, unbearable unemployment rates, substandard health care, and severe shortage in housing).

The slaughtered were still in their civilian clothes, their bodies are burnt, and their identities are kept unknown.

Those bodies will rot and burn by military orders even though all are unidentified.

General **Mohamed Ibrahim** announced the death of 42 people nationwide.

Falsification of records of killed civilians by military, police, and government officials is routine since the 1952's military coup by Nasser against King Farouk.

Here, in the mosque of Rabaa, the toll was two thousands; many bodies were transported to nearby clinics and mosques that belong to private people.

191

The cell phones in the hands of every living person conveyed to the world this grim scene of dead civilians, never carried armed, still in their civilian dresses, never have expected to face lethal weapons.

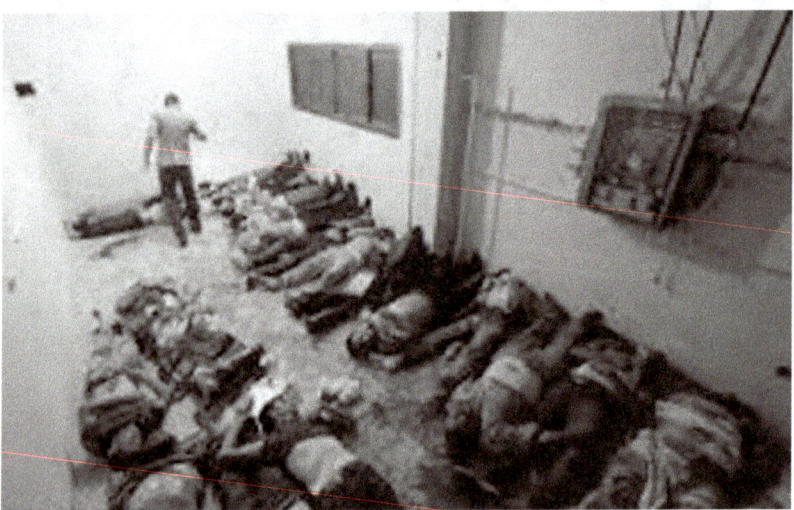

In the mosque of Rabaa Al-Adawiya, dead bodies are laid to rot at room temperature. The major city **Morgue of Zenhum** already has long waiting lines.
There are no means to transport the bodies out of the square.

Those are not actors in a bloody movie.

Those are civilian Egyptians slaughtered on August 14, 2013 by Abdul Fattah El-Sissi's coup army.

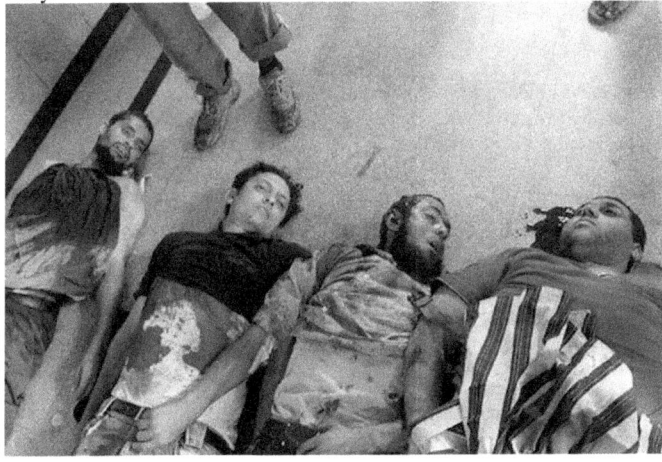

Four young men still bleeding fresh blood.

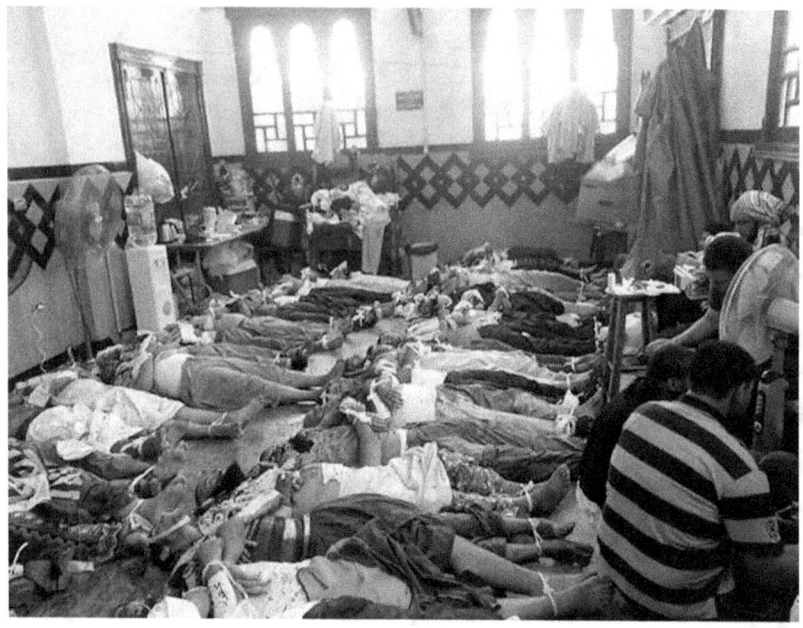

This is the hall of praying of Rabaa Al-Adawiya mosque which will be burnt over the dead by the Egyptian military.

Some of those dead were transformed to the basement of the platform of the speaker (where they preached Islamic speeches) by the police for the purpose of fabricating legal evidence to accuse islamists by murder in the basement of the platform.

They came here from every village in Egypt to uphold the words of God and protest the military coup.

They were shot dead, burnt, or run over by the vehicles of their own army and police.

The police was able to use water hoses or wait few months until campers exercise their civilian rights to protest or run out of supplies.

Tying the lower jaw to the skull the two feet, and the two hands allows transferring the dead body without getting limbs or tongue fall out or violating the sanctity of human body. The tongue is prevented from showing outside the mouth; the limbs are restrained from falling outside the carrying boards or sheets of cloths.

Some dead were tied at hands and ankles; few have their lower jaws tied to their skulls.

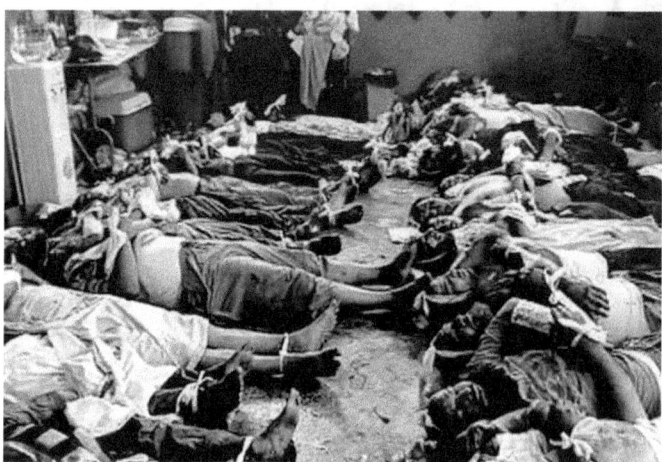

There are few thermoses that might contain some ice, but the number of dead bodies is too large to fill state official morgues.

Stench of dead bodies conveyed to the chronicles of history, not to catch the killers, but to alter society so that man's conscience should never again let that happen.

General Abdul Fattah El-Sissi broadcast a meeting with the Egyptian Army officers on the issue of selling cars to the 160,000 officers by mediating an affordable deal of monthly payments. As the highest authority in Egypt, El-Sissi might never sense the damage he inflicted on his image and on the country by exposing his shallow personality. **There is no one on his sides.** He alone runs all debates. The audiences are military personnel, could not speak, or even applaud without his permission.

Frequently, he would say "**I am talking seriously**", as if he does not think the audience believes him. He then shouts and threatens any officer who treats lower ranks without respect.

This video seems to address his desire to show the public that he is a loving and respectful person. Yet, his slang and inability to plan his speech, made him treat his officers as elementary school kids. **Tough love** comes with shouting, threatening, and then expressing extreme affection.

After telling his officers that he cannot subsidize a 100,000 Egyptian pound car ($15,500.00), he explained that they were not in Qatar and he has no money to pay. Thus, they must buy what they could afford. He then raised the issue of giving cars away, they take them **re-sell them** for cash.

The most improper story was narrating the insults of his boss while working in Matrouh, west Egypt. His superior walked in his office, noted metal pins stuck in an eraser, told him that he was a rotten officer. He responded by saying: '**Thank you sir, God forgives you.**" El-Sissi then said that he was able to curse his superior by his mother, and other stuff, but he did not. Claiming that God rewards good behavior.

CHAPTER 8

Islamic Jihad

8.1. The Duty of Jihad

Islam was born and flourished on **Quran** as a **constitutional legislature** for mankind to uphold.

Consequently, the enhancement of personal skills in the vocalization and articulation of over 6000 verses, each embodies an idea, created constant appearances of **revolutionists and rebels** throughout the history of Islam.

The arrival of gun fire and remotely effective weapons during the **French Invasion** of Egypt in 1798 AD caused a setback in Islamic rebellion overcome by the lethal and effective modern weaponry. That was followed by widespread British colonialism of Islamic nations, also equipped with modern weaponry in face of poorly armed Islamic leaders. .

The rise of **anti-colonialism and liberation** movements against western occupations shifted the oppression powers from foreign occupiers to national military armies. Those implemented the same weaponry in oppressing Islamic ideas and skills, advanced personal greed and enriched the few who have control on the resources of weapons and conscripts (compulsorily enrolled for service, especially in the armed forces; a draftees).

The hiatus imposed on the Islamic revolution by the arrival of modern weaponry resulted into a **state-organized enslavement** of the most impoverished conscripts of the police and military exposed to the most brutal state oppression, rejected by the public, and deprived from the basic human rights of education, housing, health care, or dignified future.

In the Egyptian experiment, those who cannot read or write or memorize or recite Quran are enlisted in security state police. There, they are enslaved in the most humiliating government-controlled organization. **Muslim Brothers** were banned from joining the military, viewed as threat to military doctrine of strict adherence to law and order.

Within half a century after the rise of anti-colonialist liberation movements and the ensuing of state-conscripted army and police, many wars imposed high tolls on the lives of conscripts. In 1967 war between Egypt and Israel, thousands of lives were lost. The top leaders of the Egyptian military was neither qualified to manage national security, nor known for leading the life of responsible state officials.

General **Abdul Hakeem Amer** (Chief of Staff of the Egyptian Army 1956–1967) and **Salah Nasr** (head of Egyptian Intelligence from 1957-1967) were two among the most corrupt state officials during Nasser's regime. Amer was either executed or committed suicide, Nasr was imprisoned. Both men engaged in sex and drug scandals, dereliction of duty that led to the 1967's defeat of Egypt. Both men devastated the future of Muslim Brotherhood, caused many of Islamists to flee Egypt during 1960's, many imprisoned or executed. Both men joined the Egyptian Military Academy which graduated Nasser, Sadat, Mubarak, and El-Sissi.

Heikal told stories about how Salah Nasr, while visiting India, learned the Indian ritual and erotic sexual use of cannabis as the sacred crop. Nasr coached Amr on those rituals. Nasr is also blamed for providing Amr with poison for committing suicide. Amr was known of his many sex partners among the Egyptian actresses.

Warda Al Jazairia   Berlanti Abdel Hamid

Warda Al-Jazairia was an Algerian-Lebanese singer discovered in sex affair with Egypt's deputy and defense minister, Abdul Hakim Amer. Berlenti Abdul Hamid married Abdel Hakim Amer over his first wife. Whether either woman was spy on the Egyptian military will never be known. But, they succeeded in getting their shared man killed.

After the 1967 defeat, **Abdul Hakeem Amer** was either killed or forced to commit suicide, but the damage to the military defeat lingered to this date. Similar tragic losses of lives occurred in Iraq's **Saddam Hussein**'s army between 1979 and 2003. That led to hanging Saddam and few of his relatives and top leaders in the same time.

After the massive plundering of national resources by the national anti-colonial movements and the failure to support or plan for the growth and security of statehood, a cascade of revolting movements comprising the **Arab Spring** ignited in Tunisia, Libya, Egypt, Yemen, Syria, and Sudan.

Clearly, Islamic orators and vocalists are now being outnumbered by massive military and police machines equipped by the most advanced American technical warfare. The **militarization of islamists** which led to the 1952 revolution by Gamal Abdul Nasser was set back by Nasser's ingenious rejection of the **islamic project** for the sake of advancing his own social agenda.

As will be seen later, Mohamed Morsi did not grasp that experience from Nasser, stuck with the Muslim Brothers and ended up by losing power. But, Nasser's abandonment of the Muslim Brothers threw him in the bed of secular military fellows, who would later plunder Egypt beyond any hope for securing a viable statehood.

For half a century, the course of militarization of islamists has been hindered by the most delusional groups of **Ben Laden** and **Ayman Zawahiri**. The two conferred bitter taste to Islamic Jihad by acting on their immediate impulses and anguish towards the governments that oppressed them. Zawahiri was persecuted repeatedly by all Egyptian governments, Ben Laden by

201

Saudi governments. Both men were rightfully seeking change of governments that oppressed their peoples, yet with a twist of detached flavor of utopian Islam.

The narrow, linear, and constricted views of Zawahiri and Ben Laden were confronted by equally mindless aggression from the Egyptian and Saudi governments. Indeed, the standoff between radical Salafi fundamentalists and totalitarian Saudi and Egyptian authorities left most muslims in disdain from the inflexibility of islamists and thuggish rulers.

The fortunate chasm between moderate and businessmen of Muslim Brothers, on one side, and fundamentalist and secluded Salafis of **Jihad Salafi**, on the other side, must intersect at the cross road of gaining military power.

On January 31, 2011, Muslim Brothers succeeded in opening the Egyptian prisons and letting loose thousands of oppressed and improperly imprisoned islamists. That was followed by launching aggressive election campaign that ended by capturing the presidential power in Egypt.

As the vocal and orator Jihad Salafis breathed relief and many of them returned home after many decades in alienation of their own homeland, the **Muslim Brothers** made the fatal error of losing sight of Mubarak's remaining men in every branch of the government.

The partying Islamic factions that bought into the **democratic process** could not fathom the arrogance and recklessness of Mubarak's men. Those possess total control over the military and police power. The vocal and orators of Salafis and Muslim Brothers exploited their slogans to the extreme without planning, by the means of Islam, to counter the reverse revolution of Mubarak's men. Those have a full year to organize and sabotage every function of the newly elected Islamist and president.

This time in history, the internet and electronic communication placed islamists under the spot light. Plenty of islamists could not still restrain or balance their eloquent recitations of heavenly verses of Quran with their **immediate means to change reality**. Some of those could not comprehend the fact that guns, bullets, conscripts, and resources are the rules of the game.

Some islamists reckoned on the fact that the critical mass of people mistrusting secular corruption for sixty years might do away with direct fighting combat. In such cross roads between the **power of persuasion** and **power of bullets**, some leading islamists demonstrated the most detached style of reckoning on heavenly power to carry on their threats and promises.

Another sect that was threatened daily by annihilation by the Israeli and American powers in Gaza, Afghanistan, Iran, Syria, and Iraq, learned to plot and manufacture their own weapons in preparation for final battles.

8.2. Abroad Protests

Exiled muslims in western countries found the opportune moment to express their hidden suffering that led them to leave their homeland searching for better life abroad.

Egyptian flags and crowds outside Egypt conveyed to the world the realities of corruption in Egypt. **The people have spoken.**

Even protesters overseas failed to deter General Abdul Fattah El-Sissi from committing massacres against his own people. El-Sissi sought immunity as a condition for retiring from the military to run for presidency, realizing that as soon as El-Sissi turns civilian he would be sued, tried, and probably hung for murdering six thousand Egyptians.

Tunisia started the Arab Spring first, thus snatching the honor of liberating its people from Egypt. This led the Arab revolutionary liberation in 1952, felt its lost lure in the Middle East. Egypt woke up in roar, anger, and determination to rewrite history.

8.3. Tit For Tat

Egypt's Defense Minister Gen. **Abdel Fattah Al-Sissi** (center), Prime Minister **Hazem Al-Beblawi** (right), and army's Chief of Staff Lt. Gen. Sedki Sobhi (left) attend the funeral of Giza Police Gen. **Nabil Farrag** in Cairo, Egypt, Sept. 20, 2013.

Farrag was killed during the deployment of security forces to the town of **Kerdasa** of Giza after a massacre of its local Sheriff and 13 policemen by angry mobs taking revenge of the murders of their relatives in Rabaa Adawiya.

General Sedki Sobhi appears frightened and has never been heard or seen except in this unusual occasion. Beblawi was dragged to power against his will for fear of getting arrested with false charges. ElBaradie made sure to resign his post while being in Vienna, Austria, in order to evade arrest and imprisonment by El-Sissi's police.

الشهيد عميد شرطة « محمد جبر » مأمور قسم شرطة كرداسة

Soon after El-Sissi executed the Massacres of Rabaa Al-Adawiya, Major **Mohamed Gabr**, the Sheriff of Kerdasa Police department, in Giza, was slaughtered together with 13 police recruits.. The major general who led attack to arrest the killers of Gabr was also shot on the same ground, not necessarily by enemy fire.

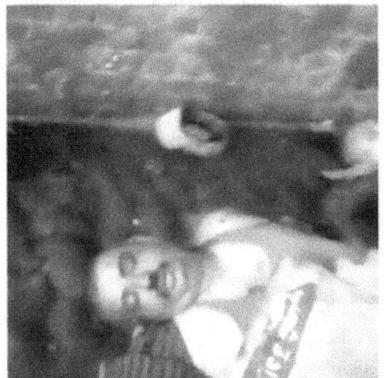
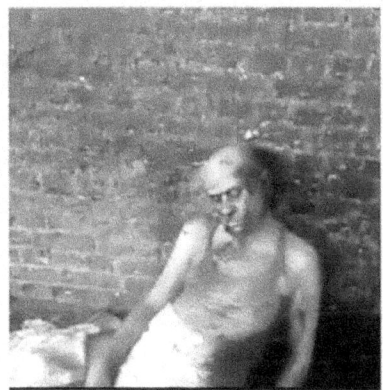

As soon as the police invaded Rabaa Al-Adawiya and slaughtered its civilian inhabitants, outraged civilians in Kerdasa, Giza, attacked the police department and slaughtered all its occupants. The sheriff and 13 policemen were dead.

The history of retribution for murder crime is strongly tied to the Bedouins' cultures that consider the human life an ultimate property of God.

Only God can give or take life, hence the murderer must be murdered.

The capital Cairo of Egypt has witnessed numerous infamous tales of such retribution for murder.

On 14 June 1800, **Jean Baptiste Kléber** was assassinated by a Kurdish muslim student, **Soleyman El-Halaby**, living in Egypt. Then, on February 20, 1910, Boutros Ghali was shot for his role in Denshawai massacre. In 1948, the prime minister of Egypt **Mahmoud Al-Nukrashi Pasha** sensed the potential and popularity of the Muslim Brotherhood in launching coup against the monarchy and government. He outlawed the Brotherhood in December 1948, leading to his assassination on 28 December 1948.

| 1800 | 1910 | 1948 | 1981 | 2013 |
| Kleber | Ghali | Nukrashi | Sadat | Ibrahim |

In the recent history, Sadat was also shot to death in Cairo, on October 6, 1981, after randomly arresting and imprisoning thousands of activists including the **Mohammad Islamboullie**, the brother of the assassin.

Not that El-Sissi and Ibrahim were statesmen performing their honorable duty to restore peace and protect state security, but because the two engaged in illegal coup and committed crimes that have never been witnessed in the Egyptian life. Those include exploding human skulls, exploding guts, mostly for civilian people engaging in civilian protests. The burning of Rabaa Al-Adawiya's mosque with dead people inside the mosque has never been committed even during Napoleon's invasion of Egypt in 1798.

Businesses suspected to belong to bearded owners were confused with those of Muslim Brotherhood were vandalized by same actors for hire.

صورة لاقتحام فيلا محافظ الفيوم واحراقها منذ قليل

In **Fayoum**, Egypt

The private villa of the governor of **Fayoum**, south west Cairo, was burned in the aftermath of the massacre of Rabaa Al-Adawiya.

In **Aswan**, South Egypt

In the wake of Rabaa Al-Adawiya massacre, the governorate building of Aswan was burned by angry rioters.

9/11 was just the beginning of theatrical violence in real life outside for the big screen. This is an Egyptian military armored vehicle catching fire on the streets of Cairo.

First suicide car attack in Sinai

It bears all features of Al-Qaeda was anticipated even before 2011. This is considered a mean to weaken the Egyptian army by funding Islamic guerilla to wage unconventional war. El-Sissi adopted the same failing tactics used by the defunct Soviet Union and the United States in

Afghanistan. Failure in Afghanistan resulted in greater expansion of religion-based militia in Africa and Asia.

On the hundredth day of the military coup, October 11, 2013, Sinai was engulfed in a fearsome simultaneous six explosions in a show of power of militant islamists.

8.4. Cairo's Resistance

Cairo's highways are the most effective places to squeeze life out of the people and out of the fragile government. The army and rioters fight over those cross sections that could shake the foundation of the hated system of police government. Note the smoke and tear-gas in **Ramses Square**, Cairo.

Joe Tube is run by a young Egyptian comedian of the style of Mohamed Fawzy Bakous. In this clip, Joe describes General El-Sissi an owl or crow that brings bad luck.

El-Sissi's foolishness drowned the Middle East in such bleak state. Tourism is destroyed, companies closed and laid workers off, killing and arrests are everywhere, military trials of civilians are held randomly, food and fuel are in severe shortage, and security is entirely lacking.

This bridge in Cairo, Egypt, passes over the most impoverished residents of the cemeteries. Those pray that they are left alone in their homelessness in sheltered cemeteries. But the rioters

213

flocking to Cairo from every village in Egypt seek more than shelters in cemeteries. If burning the capital could get the attention of the government, then this is the place to be.

Night riots became the safest way to protest and not get shot by roof snipers or photographed by cameras not equipped by night vision.

From distance, **Rabaa Al-Adawiya** is covered by smoke and tear-gas. Note, the curb that separates the street from the sideway lacks tiles or cement or bricks. The curb was removed by the campers of Rabaa Al-Adawiya to construct barriers that might slow down or impeded invading army vehicles.

The vast majority of Egyptians has no dental health care or medical health care, and most are unemployed. This man without tooth could not find any chance to voice his wishes than this occasion when all people alike share resentment for government.

Muslim women, wrapped in overhead cover, are the main victims of Egyptian oppression and corruption. Egyptian males might have chances to emigrate, seek job opportunities overseas, but women are stranded at home, either cannot find males who could afford the expenses of marriage, or their husbands have left and might never return.

Many Egyptian males left their wives and children at home, married to American women in order to obtain **greencard** that could allow them to get jobs in America, from which they could feed their families at home. In many instances, the Egyptian male married to two women, one American, the other Egyptian, is compelled to split his residency between the two nations, sometimes concealing his dual marriage from each wife and from the government. In my own experience, one of my professors in Nuclear Engineering was forced to return home with his American wife, to divorce his Egyptian wife, in order to become an American citizen.

All-women rallies are derived by the severe suffering of muslim women on the hands of ruthless corrupt government. Those are well-educated women with impeccable knowledge of Islam, history, and western values. They ask for nothing less than Islamic justice and equality. They reject western moral decay and unaccountable freedom of destruction of human decency.

In a country stricken by extreme poverty, the police is equipped by top notch tear-gas warfare equipments, purchases its tear-gas canisters from Israel. Those young men would have never been here if they were able to find jobs or have hope in the future. Unlike many unemployed or homeless people in the west, those two men have grown in many generations that suffered from marginalization by the government.

Since all European and American embassies deny visas to immigrants without financial resources, many young Egyptian men drowned in the sea while trying to reach Europe on unfit sail boats. Those who arrived safely inland of Europe face the severe rules imposed by the **European Union** of banning foreigners from jobs. Before the European Union, various European nations sympathized with immigrants and turned blind eye on their illegal employments as long as they do not cause danger to others.

Since crossing the sea on boats led to death, working illegally overseas led to homelessness, and those who get work permits in foreign nations are treated as inferior citizens, Egyptian youths learned from older bothers and relatives living overseas that **the fight must be here, in Egypt**.

All men, all ages, in August 2013's riots to protest the military coup.
Even soldiers might die from dehydration in those dark and heavy military suits.

This naïve rioter bought into the government propaganda that Islamists are terrorists. Mubarak used that excuse to gain support from the USA as the man of America against Islamic terrorism.

Mubarak's corruption placed 90 million Egyptians on the route for homelessness and despair. Even if economic reform is achieved expediently, few **generations** of illiterate and isolated Egyptians in every Egyptian village and city will still struggle with the heavy burden of poverty.

Morsi's posters is carried high by his supports and voters who elected him, not because of his great accomplishments, but because he was not helped to accomplish any thing and was kidnapped and imprisoned by military officers not elected by the people.

The state flags are not favored by Muslim rioters unless they were surrounded by police and army. Most Egyptians see the flags as signs of hypocrisy that shield the tyrant under the clout of patriotism. This crowd is paid and pushed to come here on October 6, 2013 to support the coup.

Fires are committed by many homeless people willing to commit any crime for any sum of money offered from diverse factions seeking anarchy. El-Sissi and his men benefited from fabricating terror and chaos that could be used in potential future litigation against the illegal coup and the many massacres committed since July 3, 2013. Muslim Brotherhood benefited from continuous anarchy in order to gather greater masses to undo the coup, in the same fashion used to sabotage Morsi's rule.

The invasion, destruction, and killing of Rabaa Al-Adawiya and Nahda Squares were unthinkable by any observer and in the aftermath of imprisoning Mubarak, the capture and execution of Saddam and Qaddafi, and the criminal charges filed against the Al-Basheer, the president of Sudan.

One assumes that El-Sissi would have learned that blood shed does not go with impunity.

The deep state of Mubarak orchestrated the burning of properties belong to Muslim Brotherhood, while the Interior Minister Mohamed Ibrahim refused protecting private properties from vandalism, both due to shortage in police human resources and widespread chaos that spread in all 25 providences of Egypt.

Bulldozers are backed by armored military vehicles and snipers taking places on surrounding roof tops (video taped on daily YouTube clips). Dead, wounded, and burnt civilians were deceived by tight blockage of all exits, snipers and tear-gas throwers in helicopters, and absence of any loud speakers or alarms to warn campers to leave the camp grounds.

The unthinkable scene of Egyptian army fighting on the Egyptian streets alerted the United States to cut military aid to Egypt. "We will not be doing business as usual", the American side declared. Unlike western societies, the Egyptian society depends mostly on extended families, with very little mobility of its members away from home; most people cannot separate by marriage or remote job opportunities. That renders the death of any member of the family a major issue of retribution and endless fights to deliver justice. In the case of Al-Mansoura's murder of three veiled muslim women by proxy agents of the police, the families and neighbors of the three murdered women bombed the police station was massive load of dynamite within hours of the murder of their loved ones, on July 23, 2013.. Many soldiers and officers died in the explosion for their failure to sense the local tradition of revering women as sisters, daughters, mothers, or wives that should be protected, not shot to death by police agents.

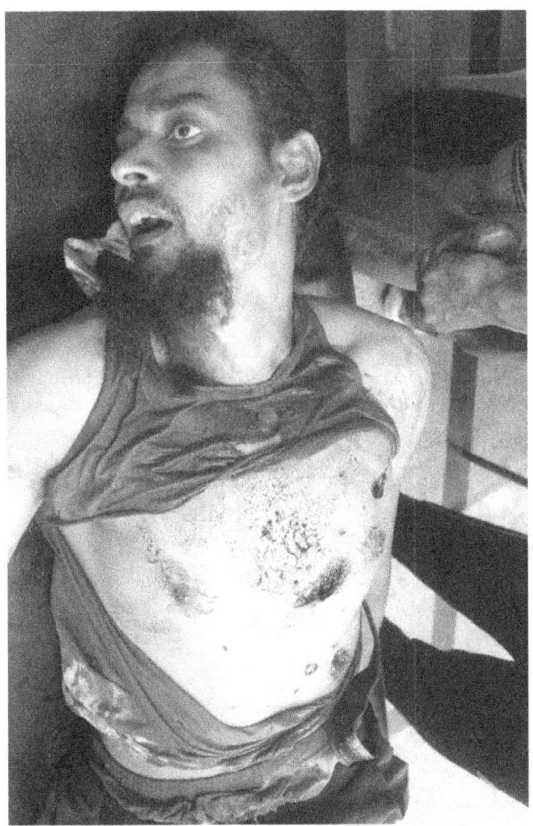

Penetrating gun shots to the chest, abdomen, and skull have claimed many lives, and all snipers, except one were never caught or punished. The only officer called the "Eye Hunter police sniper" **Mahmoud El-Shinnawy.**

Egyptian Police officer **Mahmoud El-Shinnawy**a was accused of deliberately shooting at protesters' eyes during the Mohamed Mahmoud clashes in November 2011, is sentenced to three years in prison.

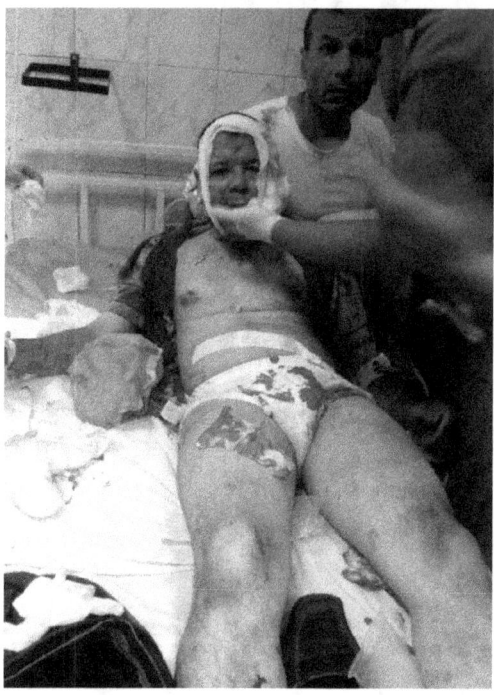

To earn living, the only job in town is getting paid to fight for one faction against the other. That included getting shot by any faction, including the one this man fought with.

This severely wounded man, who came out to rally against unemployment, hunger, and poor living conditions, is now facing more aggravating injuries which might affect even any possibility of emigrating far seeking better life.

CHAPTER 9

Exiled Islamists

9.1. Sheikh Yusuf Al-Qaradawi

Sheikh **Yusuf Al-Qaradawi** is an outlawed Muslim Brother and Egyptian citizen, fled Egypt in 1961 and took refuge in Qatar. He is now Qatari citizen.

Like the majority of muslims, the sheikh sanctioned resistance to Israeli occupation of Palestine and American occupation of Iraq. Thus, he was outlawed by the United States and by Egypt. He was jailed in Egypt three times before his fleeing.

Al-Qaradawi echoed the same claims made by millions of sane people, that an elected president should not be removed by his subordinate military officers. He went to the extreme to ask all jihadists from allover the world to travel to Egypt and fight against El-Sissi.

"I call on Muslim throughout the world in every place, in Indonesia, Malaysia, Nigeria . . . India, Somalia, Iraq, Iran . . . and in every country of the world, I call upon them to do Shahada' [witnesses or martyrs]."

Even though, like thousands of Muslim Brothers and Islamists, **Yusuf Al-Qaradawi** was chased, arrested, and imprisoned three times by Nasser's regime of Egypt, and even though he fled Egypt to avoid further imprisonment or execution and to seek safe and free life in Qatar, yet the sheikh invites all others to travel to Egypt and take Shahada, to **fight and die in support of Islam**.

226

Like many others Islamic authorities, such demonstration of selfishness and treating others as unworthy to the same safety and freedom afforded to them posed concern to his critics.

But, the sheik does not speak plain empty wisdom. In Islam, the levels of Shahada are many. Some people could support Islam in their hearts, some by words, and some by hand, some by weapons, other by life.

In his 67, Al-Qaradawi could not endure the murder of 52 prayers in front of the Presidential Palace, the massacres of Rabaa Al-Adawiya or Nahda squares. In his Fatwa or religious edict, he sought the withdrawal of Abdel Fattah Al-Sissi and the restoration of **legitimacy and democracy**.

"I call on Al-Sissi and those with him and all parties and political powers in Egypt to stand united to defend the truth and reinstate President Morsi and to continuously advise him."

He also criticized Al-Azhar Grand Sheikh Ahmed Al-Tayyib for supporting coup against the legitimate President of the country, saying his stance is neither supported by the Quran nor Hadeeth (speeches and deeds of Prophet Muhammad other than Quranic verses).

Qaradawi stated that Coptic Pope **Tawadros II** "was not authorized to speak in the name of Copts," nor was Mohamed ElBaradie delegated by Egyptians to speak in their name. ElBaradie only has the support of a handful of people and the opposition has not said that he is their representative.

Qaradawi stressed that the ouster of the first elected president in Egypt was wrong both constitutionally and jurisprudentially.

"A president who was undoubtedly elected through democratic means should serve his entire term of four years so long as he is capable of working."

On June 30, 2013, millions of Egyptians flocked to the streets across Egypt to demand Morsi's ouster and early presidential elections. Qaradawi's son, Abdel Rahman Yusuf, wrote a letter to his father explaining Morsi's exclusion of non-Muslim Brothers.

Like Senator John McCain and million others, Al-Qaradawi explained that the June 30 riots were plotted by Mubarak's regime; Morsi was prevented from ruling by the failure of the army and police to enforce the laws, and the corrupt judicial system that let wrong doers walk free.

Al-Qaradawi wrote to a number of international bodies calling for the Arab League, the UN, and the African Union, among others, to "take a stance" toward the deposing of Morsi and "to come to Egypt and see what is happening" there.

Qaradawi reprimanded Al-Sissi for calling for massive demonstrations on July 26, 2013, to delegate to him mandate to fight with "terrorism". Massive demonstrations are not performed under judicial oath or supervision and have never been accepted as tool of democratic processes.

Qaradawi condemned the Sheikh Ahmad Al-Tayyib, for having supported the coup against Morsi.

9.2. Sheikh Wagdi Ghoneim

Sheikh Wagdi Ghoneim is a younger generation of Muslim Brothers from those of Al-Qaradawi. He served in the Egyptian Army, jailed eight times, fled Egypt, and finally settled in Qatar.

Ghoneim comprises a characteristic brand of islamists. He gathers the charisma of a man bent of higher virtues of heavenly justice, the secular attitude of reckless and impulsive sarcasm and jokes. That both entertains and when improperly situated diminishes the stature of the joker. Ghoneim used excessive slang epithetic in mixes of curses, prayers, and wishful demands.

Ghoniem's service in the Egyptian Army and his long and indefinite exile away from home turned him onto fearsome antagonist to the military coup. Even though Ghoneim possesses such unique inclination of making Quranic canons as objective as an objective mind wishes to construct, his poor academic education blocked his progress beyond wishes, curses, prayers, and plenty of light humor entertainment.

Indeed, Wagdi Ghoneim was blessed for his sequestration from western indoctrination in superficial objective philosophies. Unlike Mohamed ElBaradie who obtained his doctorate in law from the United States and exhibited completely alien mindset to Egyptian and Islamic philosophies, Ghoneim viewed Allah as living supreme power that must be called in all political and human conflicts.

Ghoniem's wishes came true as Egypt burnt in tragic and ceremonial senses that could finally break the backbone of long ingrained corruption, injustice, and extreme inequalities.

Despite Ghoneim's irritating persona to many conservative Islamists, his personal suffering and never-ending exile gather the sympathy of millions of Egyptians in sensing the solemn value of having a state of their own.

Ghoneim was expelled from Yemen, South Africa, the United States, England, and Malaysia during his ordeal to find a country that could accept him other than Egypt. Egypt would have him arrested, imprisoned, and most probably executed due to his strong beliefs that Quranic canons should rule societies.

The basic figurative logic of Islam got Sheikh Wagdi Ghoneim to describe El-Sissi as a **car thief** who stole an automobile which he does not know how to drive. In order to appeal to the majority of impoverished peasants and urban dwellers, the new automobile requires that El-Sissi must master the vocalization of Quran and comprehend the figurative contents of its verses

If thirteen million Egyptians elected Morsi, only God could detour such fate and that El-Sissi is not greater than "Allah Is Great". Hence felt most islamists.
El-Sissi must also submit to the court of Allah, to explain how he was given the right to shoot, kill, and burn civilians in front of the Presidential Palace, in Rabaa Adawiya, and in other squares and streets.

El-Sissi must also solve the **impasse of reelecting** a new president when El-Sissi breached the Oath in front of his superior, made a superior of his own, took the Oath under his made superior, and now planning to get a newly elected superior.
Thus, Wagdi Ghoneim's depiction of the unqualified car thief is obtained directly from the Quranic logic, that a man who lies and cannot be trusted must be fought until his menace is eliminated.

Wagdi Ghoneim describes the second doctrine regarding **robbers** who robbed a house, threw owner onto the streets, and brought their own associate robbers to enjoy the booty.

Ghoneim applies the same doctrine on the Zionist occupation of Palestine, which replicated the 11th century crusades on Jerusalem. The owner of the house might have been taken by surprise and allowed the robbers to occupy their property, as El-Sissi did to Morsi. Ghoneim explains the ensuing consequences of committing wrongs and supports that by the Quranic canons of fighting the unjust liars and dishonest enemies until peace is restored.

Ghoneim describes the ongoing civilian and armed rebellions against El-Sissi and his military coup, as seeking the ultimate justice of hanging El-Sissi and restoring legitimacy of law and order of elected government.

Ghoneim's many **shrewd interpretations** of Quranic verses are attributed to his vast life experiences rather than education. Ghoneim was raised and nurtured by Muslim Brotherhood which comprised of many good and well-mannered men. Those could guide youth to straight path and disciplined life. Like most Muslim Brothers, Ghoneim resented the hypocrisy of Azhar's men and launched constant criticism on its corrupt clerks.

Exceptionally, Ghoneim was allowed to the military as a reserve officer after 1973 after his graduation from the school of commerce. When Sadat rounded all islamists and imprisoned them, Ghoneim waited for the first chance to flee Egypt and never to return. As Ghoneim describes his life in exiles, he cites the famous Islamic wisdom:

"If they imprison me, I am free in my solitude.
If they expel me, I am free in God's vast refuge.
If they kill me, I will be free in the heaven of my creator."

Indeed, Ghoneim roamed God's refuge from Egypt, Italy, Belgium, England, USA, Yemen, South Africa, Malaysia, Lebanon, and ended up in Qatar. That gave Ghoneim great exposure to very diverse cultures.

Ghoneim admits in one of his interviews that he lifts weights to keep in shape. That is almost entirely unheard of in muslim Imams, most of those who lack touch with worldly matters beside their close world of rehearsing the same repeated stuff in religious books. Hence, Ghoneim possesses such acute sense of humor and ability to bring Quranic verses to the immediate state of **objective inquisitive minds**.

That however did not prevent Sheikh Ghoneim from falling in the morbid habit of cursing, swearing, and indulging in wishful and futile rhetoric that taint him as an out-of-touch parroting demagogue.

In fact, once the constant ability to learn (and expose to new problem-solving challenges, such as emigration, physical suffering, and engaging activities) most people, not only clergies, succumb to the **perils of stagnation**, boredom, ignorance, and irrationality.

The reverse argument is also valid, in that many isolated minds could **retain sense of purity** and lack the distraction of peer pressure and insidious slipping into the quagmire of irreversible cultural and moral decay. For example, Salafis viewed democracy as a sort of "Kufer" or opposition to God's canons which imply that only pious and straight people should lead. Democracy brings the most liked individual.

Salafis might have missed the concrete fact that Mohamed Morsi was both pious and straight and was elected democratically. Yet, Salafis have definitely missed the glaring alarms in Quran that the forces of evil will always prevail if not opposed by greater power of terror and arms.

Ayman Zawahiri and many Salafi leaders stressed the inevitable armed Jihad as the only tool of change. The Iranian revolution did not achieve its goals by appeasing the Shah or the superpowers, but succeeded through the death of two million martyrs and after thirty years of oppression.

Now, the Salafis have to meddle with the unshakable paranoia of the military rulers who could not even learn from history, that tanks, armored vehicle, airplanes, and imprisoning opponents would only enrich the few men on the top of the military coup, while an entire nation of ninety million oppressed people would turn into uncontrollable anarchy for generations to come.

9.3. Youssef Moustafa Nada

Youssef Moustafa Nada was born in Egypt in 1931, belongs to the same generation of Youssef Al-Qaradawi. Nada shared with Qaradawi the same fate of Muslim Brothers during Nasser's era. He fled Egypt through Libya and finally settled in Switzerland and earned its citizenship.

Nada is an example of businessman of Muslim Brotherhood who succeeded in escaping oppression in Egypt and built a financial empire in Europe. The United States accused Nada by financing the activities of al Qaeda, charges he vehemently denied.

Youssef Moustafa Nada is an example of exceptional businessman of Muslim Brotherhood.

Youssef Nada suffered in the military prisons of Nasser in the 1960's. A true eyewitness to the brutality of tyrannical oppression.

After becoming a wealthy and connected figure, Youssef Nada paid for the airplane that transported Ayatallah Khomeini from Paris, France, to Tehran on the dawn of the Iranian Revolution. A decade later, he interfered to Saddam Hussein during the 1991 war with Kuwait as a peacemaker and as the de facto foreign minister of the Muslim Brotherhood.

After half a century in exile, Nada has been involved in all aspects of the 'Arab Spring' in Egypt, including the elections in which the Muslim Brotherhood got to power. Islamic conviction put this man at odds with many governments throughout the Arab world. He is international political foreign emissary of Muslim Brotherhood.

Nada believes that Muslims religious scholars have not used their brains since the 12th Century that ruling Muslim states by inheritance is a betrayal of Islam and Muslims, and that Palestine and Israel as two states will never work.

Thus, Nada married the practical capitalistic philosophies of accumulating wealth as the ultimate tool to power with his utopian Islamic beliefs that God's justice cannot be defeated. He jokes about irony of dry souls in a tale that took place in the military prison in Egypt. A fellow blind Muslim Brother in his 80's, was imprisoned with Nada in the same ward. Every time the jailer beat the blind elderly prisoner, the old man prays that God spares their eyes and save their children from getting harmed. Nada laughs in sarcasm on the contrast of ruthless and ignorant jailers versus helpless and pious blind elderly man.

The ignorance of the illiterate jailer, who was not privileged with learning the Quran, and the tranquility and tolerance of the blind elderly man blessed with the comforting power of heavenly justice, never left Nada's conscience.

The two were engraved in his acute sense to knowledge and faith.

CHAPTER 10

Egyptian Copts

10.1. Christian Colonialism

The industrial revolution in Europe equipped European Christians with weapons and hardware that helped Christians displace the Ottomans from the Middle East. Since 1798, the Middle East was the main target of European Christian occupation.

The new realities of scientific progresses in the twentieth century widened the economic disparities among the major colonial European powers. Ancient religious animosities flared up in Europe. Hence, the first half of the twentieth century was consumed in scientific competitions, military confrontations, and two major **world wars**.

The two world wars led to the collapse of **British Empire** and the liberation of many occupied colonies such as India, Iran and the Arab nations including Egypt.

The wounded and aging lion would be soon replaced by younger and mighty beasts.

Only in 1954 when Nasser sought the Soviet help to ward off the hostilities of western Christians.

The Orthodox Eastern Christianity of Russia was thus balanced with the new American and European Christianity. Not that either east or west cared about religion, but that Christian and **Islamic mindsets** and **end-games** are contradictory to each other.

In the United States, the fight to end racial segregation started the **Civil Right** movements in the second half of the twentieth century. Thus, the ancient spiritual ideologies of **Islam**, **Buddhism**, and **Hinduism** competed in displacing Christianity out of most of the ancient world.

Many Indians equated Christianity with the white men of British occupation, a foreign power that oppressed and exploited India.

In reverse, many white Americans started viewing Hinduism a utopian relief from materialism. Yoga proliferated in most American towns and villages. Pilgrims to India became fashion for many white people struggling with psychiatric problems.

Egypt, Syria, and Lebanon harbored most of the remains of ancient Christians. In Palestine, both muslims and Christians were expelled out of their land by Zionist Jews in the 1948's war between Arabs and Zionists.

In Egypt and Iraq, Christians were protected by two oppressive tyrannical governments that kept peace among the impoverished and oppressed by oppressive military means designed to help the thieves plunder, keep the sheep checked.

As soon as Saddam's secular regime collapsed in 2003, Christians started leaving Iraq. Similar waves of exodus of Christians from Syria to Lebanon took place as Bashar Asad started and continued killing Syrians and destroying his own country since 2011.

10.2. Christian Nationalism

The evolving Egyptian revolution, which coincided with the 1948's war to date, aimed at restoring the **Islamic identity** to Egypt.

For good or for worse, Egyptian Christianity or Coptic Christianity is shielded from **criticism**, constructive or otherwise, by the sensitive state between Muslims and Christians.

All Muslims could do is ward off claims of persecution of Copts or even try hard to prove that they protect, help, and support Copts. On the Coptic side, Copts try not to expose the negative features of their religions in order to avoid looking weak in front of Muslims. In addition, the Egyptian government must show to the world that it can protect the Coptic churches and treat the Copts equal with Muslims.

Thus, unlike the aggressive criticism and fighting over **Christian doctrines** in Europe, Egyptian Christianity is sheltered or quarantined, like a spoiled child living a contested divorce of his parents. Each parent tries his or her best to please the child. The scenes of Copts rallying on the streets of Cairo, Al-Menia, or Asyout with massive crosses, chanting "Live the Cross" were only seen the west in movie depicting the remote past.

In many cities in Asyout, Al-Menia, and Cairo, Copts erect huge crosses and signs to mark Coptic territories. Not that Muslims do not post large religious banners or mark streets or cities with religious marks, but that Islamic banners do not sanction symbols or pictures but meanings and values.

In the same fashion that Egypt sheltered the **Pyramids** and **Sphinx** from the elements of nature, Egypt quarantines Coptic Christianity in its pure state from the Dark Ages. In the main time, Muslim Brothers are either imprisoned and hung or fled outside Egypt. Those fled expanded Islamic ideas. Copts who migrated to the west or to Australia did no more than living in cultures that already rejected Christianities.

Coptic priests engaged in criminal acts of hiding and eliminating any Coptic converts to Islam, performing bizarre rituals of baptism detailed into 36 washing of naked bodies by "Myron" (special formula used by Coptic churches) and imposing political views on their followers. Those could still be considered internal matters within religious sects which should not concern muslims. However, in the process of democracy, almost all Coptic priests and leaders fought any Islamic agendas or islamists no matter what contents islamists could bring.

Still, that should not concern muslims, since Copts have the right to defend their own interests. The inevitable confrontation between Copts and muslims ensued after the June 30, 2013's coup. The coup comprises a major breach to all Islamic canons necessitating armed Jihad against Egypt's own army and police. Islamists are now facing the darkest forces of ignorance and oppression of their own military and police apparatuses, together with the darkest of powers of Orthodox Christianity founded mainly on abusing the illiterate and impoverished Christians.

هل يجوز للكاهن بعد رشم الأعضاء بالميرون الـ 36 رشم

Focusing attention on the Coptic practices and debates on whether the priest should spray "Myron" beyond the thirty-six described naked body parts that are usually sprayed by priests, created antagonistic reactions in the local communities in Egypt. **Bassem Youssef**, the TV host who exposed those practices, alerted people to the danger of keeping religious activities from being exposed to the public.

Concealed traditions comprised threat on education and participation in diverse society. Prior to that TV show, most Islamic rituals were publically exposed, ridiculed, and criticized for educational purposes. That was not so for Coptic rituals.

Like must Christians, Egyptian Copts dread and resent any notion to Islam, Muhammad, or Allah in an emotional sport of competition blinded to any consequences of importing western secularism to Egypt.

Soon after Morsi was ousted, gas stations started selling gasoline, electric power supply returned to normal, all islamic media outlets banned and islamists imprisoned. **Nagib Sawiris**, a Coptic billionaire then admitted that he supported people dumping oil in the desert in order to cause public anger against the government for fuel shortage.

Sawiris went to the extreme to declare on TV that if a Coptic woman converts to Islam, the law gives him the power to kill the converted woman.

In Egypt, the war between the **two philosophies** (Christianity and Islam) is not only based on the past European colonialism that favored Copts over muslims, but also on the irritating Christian symbols that invoke illiterate and impoverished muslims. The majority of those view the Trinity sign of Christianity a gross violation of trust, faith, and distortion of God's canons.

Even though the vast majority of muslims might not adhere to most rituals of Islam and care less about matters that do not intrude on their **survival needs** such as food, shelter, security, education, and health care, yet a Christian symbol wakes up the sleeping elephant.

235

The use of the word "Son" by Copts annoys muslims. Muslims view the Son as use of religion to empower priests to claim heavenly power. The use of the word "Father" enforces the same concept of substituting God by humans.

Still, pictures and crosses do not suffice to annoy muslims from Coptic tradition to the extent of warring against each other. The fact that Copts lack the wealth of Quranic words and vocals make Copt defendants without their lawyers facing a court of Quranic canons, established to free man from all mediators to God.

A muslim imam, sheikh, or claimed expert in Islam, cannot claim status over any person who could refute a false assertion by a hypocritical **trader in religion**. The examples of sheikh Ahmed Tayyib and Ali Goumaa, both were top moftis of Al-Azhar, show that muslims harbor great suspicion to sheikhs hired by despots to fool unwary followers of Islam.

This Coptic Church named "**The Franciscan Fathers**" was burned in the aftermath of Rabaa's massacre in a state of national chaos and absence of police forces in most Egyptian towns.

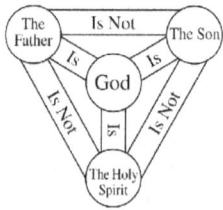

Christian Egyptians, or Copts, are thus entangled in a historic war not less brutal than that faced Jews in the Middle East.

236

Burning and loitering churches was always blamed on Muslim Brothers as a way to imprison them on criminal charges. **Habib Al-Adly**, the interior minister of Mubarak, played that card very well by getting his men to burn churches. Adly convinced Mubarak to justify the national emergency law that ruled Egypt for 30 years.

Even though many factions have interests in burning churches, most Egyptian churches entice vandalism by their rich and flashy contents in many impoverished neighborhoods. Egyptian churches look like highly secured castles always kept locked up and empty except in funerals or weddings or during Sunday services.

In contrast to churches, all mosques in Egypt are left open throughout the 24 hours of the day in order to serve the five daily prayers, mosques are left open at night for mediations, teaching, and support of the homeless.

The traditional belief that mosques are houses of God, and God alone will protect them, is behind the tradition of leaving mosques open.
Even mosques that left cash or valuables on premises are vandalized, for many believe that the money that a mosque has is better spent on needy people than on God. Or, that **God needs no money**, his creatures do.

The fact that Muslims bury their dead under the soil wrapped in white sheets, without gaskets, makes many muslims believe that Christians are insensitive to their community. The majority of impoverished muslims could not even afford the price of wood of gaskets that could provide them food, shelter, and survival necessities.

Most Coptic cemeteries in Egypt are identical to those in the west, plenty of marble, statues, gaskets, and sometimes valuable properties kept with the buried dead.

None of that would concern muslims if not that many muslim cemeteries are used as permanent **camp grounds** for homeless families.

Many of Cairo's muslim cemeteries have permanent tents, with stolen electric lines, water delivery, and make-shift bathrooms and many people were born and grown homeless in cemeteries. The legendary tales that cemeteries are haunted by the ghosts of dead people helped homeless people inhabit cemeteries out of their dire needs, while scared others away by those floating ghosts.

Burning churches and businesses is being joked of as the best way to hide financial scandals. For many unemployed people and those with life-long history of homelessness and despair, churches could be the easiest places to plunder and never get caught, or even getting paid by politically motivated agencies interested in embarrassing the government.

South Egypt has always been the graveyard for police officers. In the era before 1952, the south was oppressed by brutal wealth landlords. All peasants were enslaved by the wealthy owners, never been compensated by money for their work in farming. At the end of full-day of work, the most a peasant could get was peaces of bread and few green leaves or beans.

Trading in **opiates** and **hashish** was the major source of income in place of brutal farming labor. Since 1952, the animosity between civilians and police has been a national concern. Burning and vandalizing Coptic churches in the South Egypt suffices to punish the local police staff by major replacements and constant renewal. The new police replacements repeat the same old mistakes. That helps drug traders stay ahead of the security forces.

In the era of cell-phones, this dramatic burning of churches serves the purposes of the actors whose main interest is to get the attention of the government to take the south seriously. In fact, that tactic accomplished its intended goal and led to fast development of the south, rather than grapping all resources by the Capital, **Cairo**.

The appearance of suddenly enriched billionaires during Mubarak's regime shifted the power of funding in favor of anti-islamists. The Coptic TV Channel "**Christian Dogma**", financed and supported by billionaire **Nagib Sawiris**, sponsored Islamophobe **Ibrahim Issa**, with one definitive goal of instigating sectarian violence.

Issa's unsightly outlook or his nasal sniffing voices were not all that repulsed people from his show. Every few minutes of his show, Issa could not resist cursing, accusing, and fabricating charges against Muslim Brothers.

Because Ibrahim Issa was not nurtured or versed in Quranic vocalization or figurative verses, his show became the most comical TV in Egypt, people expected him to **devilize** islamists, Islam, and religion, and misplace repetitive adjectives in a manner never been used before and only invented by Issa out of extreme anger. An example of Issa's comical invention of Arabic expressions is his wording:

"At last, lastly, too late
Boring, slow, heavy weight, confused, random, like elephant's motion
Calcified, aged, senile.."

أخيراً أخراً متاخراً
ممل بطيء ثقيل المزن مرتبك عشواءى اشبه بحركه الافيال
متكلث مسنه عجوز

The timing of deploying Coptic antagonism to Islam, in such critical time of anarchy, prepares Egypt to the same course of internal turmoil in Iraq. Among Egyptian Copts, there are plenty of well-educated, well-mannered, and moderate intellectuals who could captivate audience by credibility, well-known peaceful and civilized traditions of Copts.

But, as we will see, even muslim intellectuals were either imprisoned or forced to flee Egypt. Those who remained behind exposed the severely polarized media in favor of the same centers of power of Mubarak.

The minister of information of Morsi's government exposed the serious fact that all Egyptian media outlets never made profits or acceptable rating, but its employers were subsidized by foreign money with astronomical salaries that compelled the TV commentators to execute foreign agendas at the expense of the national security.
A century earlier, the British occupiers of Egypt committed a massacre on June. 13, 1906, in **Denshawai**, Menufia, Egypt (north west of Cairo). In 1908, the Coptic collaborator with the British in the tribunal of Denshawai, **Boutros Ghali** became Prime Minister of Egypt. Many prominent Copts were accused of being instruments of the (Christian) British. On February 20, 1910, less than four years after his role on the Denshawai Tribunal, Ghali was shot dead in Cairo. A century latter, the grandson of Boutros Ghali, **Youssef Boutros Ghali** was sentenced to 25 years in prison as the former Egyptian finance minister. Youssef Boutros Ghali was accused for squandering public funds related to subsidized cooking gas. Ghali fled the country around the time former president Hosni Mubarak was ousted in 2011. He had already been sentenced earlier to 30 years in prison in another graft case.

Boutros Ghali, an Egyptian Copt and the grandfather of the UN Boutros Boutros Ghali, was shot to death in 1910 after being suspected for cooperating with the British occupation of Egypt in the 1906's massacre of **Dinshwayia**, Egypt (located north west to Cairo, the capital of Egypt).

Boutros Boutros Ghali, an Egyptian Copt nominated by Mubarak to the UN position, was never trusted by most muslims after his suspicious role in the war on **Bosnia** and his sanction and support of Israel's ethnic cleansing of Palestinians from their homeland.

Ghali was described by American officials as a high-handed and arrogant that alienated others. His failures of leadership during the U.N. rescue mission in Somalia and the war between Bosnians and Serbs contributed to his non-renewal for the second term. Ghali stated to **Ahmed**

Mansour of Aljazeera, on the **Epoch of Time**, that **Madeline Albright**, the state secretary of the United States, disliked him because of academic envy over professorship in international law.

Youssef Boutros Ghali, the latest grandson of Boutros Ghali and the nephew of Boutros Boutros Ghali, was sentenced, in absentia, prison for embezzlement during Mubarak's regime. He never returned to Egypt to defend his reputation.

Like his uncle Boutros Boutros Ghali, **Youssef Boutros Ghali** shared most of the qualities of his uncle Boutros Boutros Ghali described by American officials as arrogance and paranoia.

Chapter 11

El-Sissi's Strategic Vision

The student report submitted by brigadier general **Abdelfattah Said El-Sissi** in 2006 to the American War College, and is translated below, contains his understanding regarding the future of the Middle East. This is summarized as follows

1. Poverty in the Middle East is attributed to **wars** and their economic burdens on society.
2. Dictatorial governments such as Mubarak's regime (his president) controlled **media**, **imprisoned** Islamists and opponents without trials and with **fake charges**.
3. Injustice creates **terrorism** because people cannot get justice through government.
4. Democracy in the Middle East cannot succeed with economic reform and that needs **support from western democracies**.
5. Extreme groups like Hamas and Muslim Brothers will emerge through democracy and the west must allow them to rule if they are elected democratically.
6. **Corruption** in the Middle East needed specialized branches of government to assure foreign investors.
7. **Education** in the Middle East is weak and the poor economy does not encourage people to seek education.
8. The United States is suspected for intruding on the Middle East because it supported least respected governments such as **Saudi Arabia and the Gulf States**.
9. The **Army and security apparatus** in Egypt might not accept a president elected democratically who is not one among them.

Criticism

1. El-Sissi admits that **militarization** of the Middle East caused its poverty.
2. He admits that Middle **East's judicial, media, and government** systems are corrupt.
3. El-Sissi imprisoned 50 thousands of his opponents despite his knowledge **that injustice causes terror**.
4. El-Sissi claims that democracy cannot succeed without **outside help**.
5. El-Sissi toppled the Muslim Brotherhood rather than helping them perform their **democratic rule**.
6. He claims that further branches of government could **curtail corruption** without proof.
7. El-Sissi's claim that education in the Middle East is weak while imprisoning the professors and intellectuals.
8. He criticizes the American support of corrupt **Gulf Sates**, while conspiring with them to topple Muslim Brothers.
9. El-Sissi could not realize that the security and police must **protect democracy** rather than ruling the people whom they protect.

ABSTRACT

AUTHOR: BG **Abdelfattah Said ElSisi**
TITLE: **Democracy in the Middle East**
FORMAT: **Strategy Research Project**

DATE: 15 March 2006
WORD COUNT: 5127 PAGES: 17
KEY TERMS: **Middle East, Democracy, Strategic Vision**
CLASSIFICATION: Unclassified

This paper addresses the impact of democratizing the Middle East. It will assess the current **strategic and political** conditions in the Middle East and will highlight the challenge, the risks and the advantages provided by a democratic form of government. Areas addressed will include: differing perspectives between the Middle Eastern and Western cultures impacts of poverty, lack education, and religion; lack of strategic vision; **psychological nature of the people and the government**; and, inherent risks of new democracies. The paper will conclude by addressing the future of democracy in the Middle East.

DEMOCRACY IN THE MIDDLE EAST

The Middle East region is considered one of the important critical regions in the world. The Middle East region is the birth place of major religions, including Islam, Christian and Jewish religions. The effect of the **religious nature** of the environment is evident in the culture of Middle Eastern people and is one of the most important factors that affect the politics of the region. Because of the nature of the Middle Eastern culture, one must take into account the religious nature of the people when conducting diplomatic negotiations and establishing policy.

From an economic perspective, the Middle East is blessed with **huge oil and natural gas** reserves which provide much of the world's energy needs. Because of this, world superpowers maintain a keen focus on the area and attempt to influence and dominate the region so that energy requirements for economic viability within their own country are sustained (1). As a result, the Middle East is under constant pressure to satisfy multiple country agendas that may not coincide with the needs or wants of the Middle Eastern people. Furthermore, geographically and from a world perspective, the Middle East is a strategic area because of the **Suez Canal**, Straits of **Hormuz** and the **Babel Mandab** Strait. These are all critical commercial shipping lanes and are vital to any military considerations. The strategic nature of the region coupled with religious nature of the culture creates an environment that prevents challenges to the establishment of a democracy throughout the region in the near term.

The **Arab-Israel conflict** further complicates the development of democracy (2). The conflict is not strictly a Palestinian and Israeli conflict, but a conflict that affects all Arabs in the Middle East. The fact that Israel reflects a Western interest raises suspicion among Arabs about the true nature of democracy'. This, in turn, will slow the emergence of democracy in the Middle East and may justify a brand of democracy that truly reflects Middle Eastern interests and may bear little resemblance to a Western democracy (3).

Although the Middle East is beginning to transition towards democratic forms of government, there are still the remains of **dictatorial and autocratic regimes** (4). Coupled with the tension that already exists in the Middle East due to the conflicts in Iraq, Afghanistan and the conflict surrounding Israel, the conditions for further developing democracy will be strained. **The existing conflict and tension needs to be resolved before democracy can be more fully accepted by the people of the area**.

On the surface, many of the autocratic leaders claim that they are in favor of democratic ideals and forms of government, but they are leery of **relinquishing control** to the voting public of their regimes. There are some valid reasons for this. First, many countries are not organized in a manner to support a democratic form of government (5). More importantly, there are security concerns both internal and external to the countries. **Many of the nation's police forces and military forces are loyal to the ruling party.** If a democracy evolves with different constituencies, there is no guarantee that the police and military forces will align with the emerging ruling parties.

In essence the security forces of a nation need to develop a culture that demonstrates **commitment to a nation rather than a ruling party.** Furthermore, regime populations need to be prepared to assume a participatory role in a democratic form of government. This will require time to educate the population as well as develop the democratic processes that will enable democracy to gain traction.

America has been a driving force in the Middle East with respect to supporting **America's national interests.** In her effort to do so, **America has supported non-democratic regimes and some regimes that were not necessarily well respected in the Middle East. Examples include Gulf State regime, Saudi Arabia, the early Saddam regime, Morocco, Algeria, etc.** As a result, many in the Middle East question the motives of the United States and her desire to establish democracy in the Middle East now.

Is transitioning to democracy in **the best interest of United States,** or is it in **the interest of the Middle Eastern countries**? Democracy development in the Middle East will not easily emerge if the initiation of democracy in the Middle East is perceived as a move by the United States to further her own self-interest. There is also concern that the **Global War on Terrorism** is really just a mask for establishing Western democracy in the Middle East. (6) For democracy to be successful in the Middle East, it must reflect **Middle Eastern interests** and not United States' interests only. Furthermore, democracy must be seen as being beneficial to the people of the Middle East—showing respect to the religious nature of the culture as well as improving conditions for the common man. A key benchmark for testing democracy in the Middle East is how **democracy emerges in Iraq.**

Will America allow Iraq to develop in its own way as a democracy or will it try to shape democracy into a pro-Western form or regime? For example, different Muslim groups (**Muslim Brotherhood, Shia, etc.**) are likely to emerge in different Middle Eastern countries as ruling entities in democratic forms of government. If Iraq is perceived as an American puppet, then other countries may not be enticed to move towards democracy and if they do, is America ready to accept Middle Eastern democracies in their own form that may or may not be sympathetic to Western interests, particularly in the early years of a Middle Eastern democracy. The wants and desires of the countries' populations themselves need to be considered. **Do they really want democracy** and **are they willing to change their ways to establish it and make it work**? Changing a political culture is always hard. It is one thing to say that a democracy is a preferred form of government, but quite another to adjust to its requirements and accept some the risks that go along with it.

For example, history has shown that in the first ten years of a new democracy, conflict is likely to occur either externally or internally as the new democracy matures (7). The people comprising these new democracies must be committed to the democratic ideal and must be willing to overcome and work through the challenges. Simply **changing the political systems from autocratic rule to democratic rule will not be enough to build a new democracy**. The economic, religious, education, media, security and legal systems will all be affected. As a result, it will take time for people and the nation's systems to adjust to the new form of government and free market system that will emerge.

Furthermore, existing democratic countries will need to be supportive and patient with the burgeoning new democracies. In my opinion democracy needs good environment like a **reasonable economic situation**, **educated people**, and as **moderate understanding of religious issues** and at the end (minim acknowledge approved from regimes to share power). Given that the Middle Eastern countries have a strong religious base, it is important for Islamic leaders to convince the Middle Eastern people that democracy is good for the country and is not in conflict with moderate Islamic ideals.

This type of public support from religious leaders can help build strong support for the establishment of democratic systems and change that will accompany the transition. Due to the change that will be required and the accompanying time requirements, **one cannot expect the Middle Eastern countries to convert quickly to a democratic form of government**. There is a concern in the Middle East that **American is in a hurry to Democratize the Middle East** based upon its aggressive actions in Iraq and Afghanistan as well as its strategy to take pre-emptive action if she chooses to do so (8). Moving too quickly can affect the stability of the region as American motives may be perceived as **being self-centered** and not supportive of the Middle Eastern way of life. It is important that Middle Eastern countries move towards democracy in **a logical, steady and controlled manner** done on the terms of Middle Eastern countries. Yet, Western democracies will need to be supportive; providing economic, education and technological support to help foster development and change.

The Concept of Democracy from Islamic Perspective

Before continuing further, it is important to gain an understanding of how democracy is perceived by the ordinary people of the Middle East. Democracy, as a secular entity, is unlikely to be favorably received by the vast majority of Middle Easterners, who are **devout followers of the Islamic faith**.(9) Traditionally, there is tension among the Muslim countries with respect to the establishment of a democratic form of government (10). On the one hand, there are those who believe that democratic rule can co-exist with the **religious nature** of the Middle Eastern societies; however, on the other hand there are those who believe that the tribal culture of the Middle Eastern countries may not be suitable for democratic rule as too many factions will emerge. The result will be a **"fractured" society** that cannot effectively unite and there is also the risk that this could impact the **cohesion produced by the Muslim faith**.

Although concerns exist, for the most part, the spirit of democracy, or self rule, is viewed as a positive endeavor so long as it builds up the country and sustains the religious base versus devaluing religion and creating instability (11). Creating this balance will be the challenge as most Western democracies have attempted to maintain a separation of church and state. What this suggests is that as democracy grows in the Middle East, it is not necessarily going to evolve upon a Western template—it will have its own shape or form coupled with stronger religious ties.

Democracy cannot be understood in the Middle East without an understanding of the concept of **El Kalafa. El Kalafa** dates back to the time of the **prophet Mohammed** (12). During his life and the seventy year period that followed the ideal state of **El Kalafa** existed as a way of life among the people and within the governing bodies. This period of time is viewed as a very special period and is considered the ideal form of government and it is widely recognized as the goal for any new form of government very much in the manner that the U.S. pursued the ideals of "**life, liberty and pursuit of happiness**".

From the Middle Eastern perspective, the defining words governing their form of democracy would likely reflect **"fairness, justice, equality, unity and charity"** (13). Achieving the ideal is always at the forefront of the Middle Eastern society, yet following Mohammed's death and his latent influence, the government which was represented by the El Kalafa began to stray from the ideals fostered by the prophet Mohammed. The leaders of El Kalafa begin to **look inward and use power for their own well being,** rather than the well being of their fellow man. Those in power attempted to secure their power by passing on leadership control to family members rather than the most qualified leaders as determined by the members of the **Elbia,** which represented **El Kalafa** (14). As a result, dissatisfaction with how the El Kalafa process was being carried out arose, and many members became disenfranchised and chose to form their own version of El Kalafa leading to the emergence of Tribal and ethnic factions within what were once a unified Islamic body (15).

As we consider the Middle Eastern Islamic body today, we still see the fallout from the early divisions within the Islamic community, where various **tribal and ethnic factions** exist. Given this current state, the **challenge** becomes one of attempting to reunite these tribal and ethnic factions so that the earliest form of El Kalafa is reestablished. Related to the El Kalafa are the roles of the **Elbia** and **Elshorah.** Both of these processes were represented in the early years of the Muslim faith and therefore are considered important and respected processes (16). The Elbaya'a is the election process for choosing the **El Kalifa**, while the **Elshorah** advisory and oversight body to the El Kalifa or **Califate**.

The Elshorah performs its role from a religious viewpoint, in that it ensures that the Califate is carrying out his duties in accordance with Islamic teachings. Although these processes have religious historical ties, they also represent processes by which a democracy can emerge. Given the religious nature of the Middle Eastern culture, **how might a Middle Eastern democracy is structured? Will there be three or four branches of government? Should a religious branch be added to the executive, legislative and judicial branches to ensure that the Islamic beliefs and law are followed?**

A simple answer might be yes, but that is probably not the best means. Ideally, the legislative, executive and judicial bodies should all take Islamic beliefs into consideration when carrying out their duties. As such, there should be no need for a separate religious branch. However, to codify the major tenets of the Islamic faith, they should be represented in the constitution or similar document. This does not mean a **theocracy** will be established, rather it means that a **democracy** will be established built upon **Islamic beliefs.**

As one considers democracy in the Middle East, the most important action to consider is to **allow it to emerge**. It may not be the same brand or shape as Western democracy, but it will be a start.

As a general rule, most Middle Easterners fully support the spirit of democracy and will support it as long as it emerges and seeks to unify the whole. This includes allowing **some factions** that may be considered radical, particularly if they are supported by a majority through a **legitimate vote**. The world cannot demand democracy in the Middle East, yet denounce what it looks like because a less than pro-Western party legitimately assumes office. For example, the Palestinians recently elected members from the **Hamas group**. This group is not on favorable terms with the U.S. and other Western countries, yet they have legitimately elected. It is now up to the Hamas and the rest of the world to work out their political differences.

It is important that even though significant differences exist, particularly with respect to the status of Israel, that **legitimately elected** parties be given the opportunity to govern. If this opportunity is not provided, Middle Eastern countries will question the **credibility of Western nations** and their real intentions with respect to democratic rule and what it represents. At this point in the history of the Middle East, the question of democracy is an important one and the Middle East is ripe to consider it. Many in the Middle East feel that the autocratic forms of government that currently and have previously existed have not produced the progress that people expected, especially when compared to some other parts of the Muslim world, for example **Malaysia, Pakistan and Indonesia**; let alone some of the Western countries.

The question of establishing democracy is not being thwarted by Islamic tenets. The practice of Islam and democracy can coexist. When democracy was initiated in the United States, it was built upon Judeo Christian values. Given the excessive influence of the Church of England, the U.S. decided to include language in the Constitution that provided **some separation from church and state**, but religion was not eliminated from government, despite what some are led to believe.

Clearly, in the early years, religion was important and shaped the values of the American nation (17). In the Middle East, the approach is really no different with the exception that the Muslim faith is the basis upon which the Middle Eastern form of democracy will be built. As with the American tradition, other faiths would be allowed to exist, but the prevalent religion in the Middle East is Islam, so it is logical to assume that a democratic form of government will be founded on these beliefs. The challenge that exists is whether the rest of the world will be able to accept a **democracy in the Middle East founded on Islamic beliefs**. Practically speaking, this should not be an issue because

Islamic beliefs produce behavior that is more than comparable to other religious behavior.

The Middle East Democracy Challenges

Internally, there are a number of challenges that will create friction in the development of democracy. These items include the state of **poverty**, state of **education,** practice of **religion, psychological** nature of the population and the government.

Within the Middle East, the entire income is $700 billion and is less than the income of the country of **Spain**. When considering all the Muslim countries, including those outside the Middle East, the entire income is less than **France**. Poverty in the Middle East is driven by a number of factors that include **war,** for example, **Arab-Israeli conflict, Iran-Iraq war, Morocco-Es Sahara conflict and Syria-Lebanon**, to name a few. These have driven up both internal and external debt and have inhibited economic growth (18). Poor economic policies and political decisions have exacerbated the economic ills. For example, many Middle East countries attempted to sustain government controlled markets instead of free markets and as a result no incentive developed to drive the economy (19).

Government policies with respect to job creation led to difficulties because too often excess jobs were created when sufficient funding was not available to support the program resulting in **high unemployment** and public disenchantment with the government (20). Disenchant with the government is a prominent factor today and serves as a point of friction as democracy is considered

In the minds of Middle Easterners, **any government is viewed in a suspicious manner.** Furthermore, those in power seem to be living in luxury, while the common man struggles to get by. This further aggravates the perception of what government can really do for the people. Day to day people struggle to get by. The economy is not vibrant and many Middle Easterners are unemployed. Given weak economic systems, people do what they need to do to get by and often **corruption** is a path that emerges as those who hold power and wealth tends to **manipulate the poorer population** (21). As a consequence, social behavior considers this "**quid pro quo**" approach as normal. This creates cultural behavior that is contrary to the values upon which a democracy is based.

Upon implementing a democracy, there will be a strong tendency for the population to "**buy off**" their politicians in return for favors. Over time and through education this can change, but it may take a generation or two for it to happen. To address the state of poverty in the Middle East, economic and political conditions must improve whether or not a democracy is established. The fact that change is necessary creates an opportunity for democracy; however, it also creates opportunities for other forms of government as well some of which are not preferable. **Those who promote democracy do have an opportunity now in the Middle East.**

If **poverty** can be overcome in Middle Eastern countries, there can be a greater chance that democracy will more quickly emerge.

Internally, Middle Eastern countries must take action to strengthen their economies, but they are unlikely to accomplish this task without **external support from Western democracies**. Support may come in the form of investment in Middle Eastern businesses as a well as the establishment of business in the Middle East. What is important is that a commitment be made to moving the economies forward. To ensure support is being developed adequately and that precautions are taken against the **real risk of corruption, a special government agency or reporting system** should be established to regularly monitor the conduct of Middle Eastern business. Perhaps it's time to reinvigorate the role of the Arab League in economic matters trade oversight (22). These actions could ameliorate the conditions of poverty and give democracy a better chance.

As the common man in the Middle East views the billions of dollars the U.S. is spending on the war in Iraq, he may be quick to say, why don't you use that money to economically develop the Middle East instead of fighting a war? This perception suggests that economic support and stimulation may more quickly produce democratic progress. However, from the U.S. perspective, the money spent on the war is a prerequisite for establishing conditions for a lasting democracy. Without a **stable Iraq and Afghanistan**, the credibility of democracy by Middle Easterners could be questioned. Clearly, one would prefer to see billions of dollars dedicated to more peaceful economic endeavors, yet without a receptive environment economic support could evaporate.

Yet these is a need to recognize that **kinetic means** are not the only means to generate support for a stable democracy. The U.S. can be effective by seeking non-Kinetic means to build democracy in Iraq and Afghanistan. To do so, the U.S. must quickly reduce the level of fighting in the Iraq and Afghanistan and she should show support for supportive economic nations in the Middle East, such as Egypt.

The lack of a **strong education** system coupled with a **weak economy** will provide friction to the establishment of democracy in the Middle East. With the exception of Syria and Israel, the uneducated population defined as those **who cannot read or write**, approaches 30-45%.(23) **The education system is considered weak and is characterized by low attendance, poor educational materials, and limited funding,** little to no internet access (24). The education foundation is weak and its approach is considered random as it is not well connected to the Middle East's economic, governing or even religious needs. Furthermore, the overall economic system is weak and does not provide an incentive for the population to pursue education. Excessive government controls and bloated public payrolls stifle individual initiative and tend to **solidify the powerbase of ruling political parties**. In Egypt, under President **Sadat,** government controls were lifted in an effort to stimulate economic growth; however, these efforts have not blossomed under President **Mubarak**. (25) Education in the Middle East cannot be improved with only educational reforms. There must be an economic incentive that will cause the population to see the benefit of education. Therefore, educational reforms must be linked with improved economic capacity.

Those in power must also implement policies that encourage economic freedom and growth. Governing methods represented in the Middle East vary widely and include monarchies, interim government due to occupation forces, democracies, republics, a federation and a theocracy. The religious nature of the Middle East creates challenges for governing authorities, particularly under centralized control. **Governments tend toward secular** rule, disenfranchising large segments of the population who believe religion should not be excluded from government. **Religious leaders who step beyond their bounds in government matters are often sent to prison without a trial.** Those governments that claim democracy **have very tight centralized control and unfairly influence election outcomes through control of the media and outright intimidation.** When governments become **excessively powerful the oppressed may respond through terrorist acts**. The occupied territory in Israel is a good example. Because the oppression exists, a fertile environment is created that ultimately leads to extremist movements (26) There exists a moderate religious element within society, but they are not as influential as the extremists and often get associated with their misdeeds. This pits **moderate religious** elements against extremists. Because of their ability to leverage power, extremists are gaining popularity As groups, such as **Hamas** emerge, they are likely to reach power through democratic means, but they **still may not fully represent the population**, particularly the religious moderates, who they represent. So even with an elected Hamas, there are likely to be internal governance challenges down the road; however, there is hope that the more moderate religious segments can mitigate extremist measures.

The **control of the media by government** further presents problems to moderate Muslims. The media is managed via a secular philosophy. (27) The secular media secures control for the government and further **disenfranchises the religious moderates**. It spreads a philosophy of liberal living that many moderate Muslims do not support and it also **provides a vehicle for extremists to exploit** because it enables them to relate to the religious moderates on a shared theme. This has the effect of **strengthening the extremist philosophy**.

Because the government exercises excessive control over the media, **the media serves no accountability role for society as a whole** (28). If corruption exists in the government, it is likely to go unreported. As such, the masses are led to believe that their governments are good and are truly taking care of them as citizens. Yet many on the street are beginning to learn the real truth by **other means**.

The media will be an obstacle to a democratic form of government until it can be trusted to represent more than the government's perspective. This will be an immense challenge **because those in power must be willing to let go of media control**. It may be that the early stages of democracy lack **objective reporting** until independent news organizations can be established free of retribution. One the key first steps may be to initiate this approach with the help of international news organizations and pressure from democracies with free press.

Democracy risks at the current time

As mentioned earlier in the paper, the Middle East is comprised of various government types. The majority represent monarchies that **have exclusive control over their domains**. It is unlikely that these governments will voluntarily give up power any time soon in favor of a democratic means of government. Yet there is a need for some type of unifying vision that can better unite Middle Eastern countries regardless of their form of government.
Organizations such as **OPEC** and the **Arab League** are examples of organizations that represent Middle Eastern interests, but they do not serve as unifying entities such as the North African Union (29). It many be in the interest of the Middle Eastern countries to take note of government emergence in Africa as they attempt to organize on a regional basis despite differing governing means.

Given the number of monarchies that exist in the Middle East, it is no surprise that the populations look to the government for their **welfare**. Historically, this has been the case. As a general statement, the nature of **the population has been one of dependence upon and favor from the government**. Under good leadership, this has been an acceptable way of life. But under untrustworthy and corrupt leaders, the masses have had neither representation nor little to fall back on to meet their needs.

Again democracy brings challenges. Individual initiative must be fostered and rewarded so that the individual member of society can understand the importance of **pursuing their own destiny** instead of relying on the government to provide it for them. This too will take time, strong leadership, a supportive job base and economy.

Differing Perceptions Between the Middle East and Western Culture Regarding Democracy

There is hope for democracy in the Middle East over the long term; however, it may not be a model that follows a Western Template. Democracy in the Middle East must account for the wide variance of government types and it must find a unifying theme that draws the Middle East into a unified region. This where risk comes in. Presently, there is a battle raging between **extremists,** moderates and the West (30). They are each striving to exert control and establish a way of life that represents their interests.

The Future of Democracy in the Middle East

The extremists see a **Caliphate** as an ultimate goal whereas moderates are observing emerging democracies in countries like Egypt, Syria, Lebanon, and Yemen. Clearly, Palestine also has the world's attention as **Hamas** steps to the forefront.

The question arises if democracies emerge, what will they look like? I posit three options exist. The **first** is that the democracies with **an extremist bent**, like Hamas may take center stage as they effectively organize and meet the needs of the population they represent. The challenge will be whether or not they can effectively compete on the world stage without cutting themselves off from the international environment, ultimately disenfranchising their constituents. The **second form** will be in the tradition of the moderates like **Egypt or Lebanon where extremist ideologies are not readily accepted**, yet problems with **corruption** within the government are underrepresented and are not well understood by the masses. To avoid gravitating towards extremist ideologies it is important that these democracies demonstrate a better way of life for the population through representative government. The final form and least likely is the Western form of democracy.

This in an option and will serve as a model of democracy in the Middle East, but it the complexities of the Middle East are unlikely to mirror a Western image. The successful establishment of a democracy in Iraq will serve as a benchmark for Gulf State countries in the future. If it succeeds so might future moderate democracies. it will demonstrate that the multi-ethnic (Sunni, Shia) conflicts can be peacefully resolved and that they can govern in a unified manner. It will also demonstrate that democracy can resolve widespread poverty and bring about an improved **quality of life.**

Conclusions and Recommendations

Education and the **media** will be key enablers towards the establishment of democracy. There must be a shift from state controlled means to population controlled means. As media means, such as the **internet and television** become more prominent, their ability to influence education from the bottom up will tend to energize the masses. Clearly, the extremists understand the power of the media and are attempting to gain influence through their use (31). To be successful, the media must show that the moderate lifestyle is a better way. The role of religion in government will be a key issue among many. The moderate view is **that there is a place of Islamic beliefs.** Historically, for democracies including religion has been a challenge; yet this does not mean the Middle East won't succeed. A common religious understanding among all ethnicities and cultures must exist and there must be consideration given to non-Islamic beliefs.

The Middle East must view itself much in the same manner as the European Union. They represent various countries and cultures that have varying standards of living, but yet see the need to organize for the betterment of Europe—economics, security and international influence.

For these same reasons, the **Middle East should organize as a region**. This will help galvanize the Middle East as a region and may foster free market interaction which is conducive to democratic development. And finally, as the Middle East develops the rest of the world should seek ways to assist in promoting democratic values and means investing in educational means would be a good starting point.

Endnotes

(1) Zayed and the Arabic Petrol available at http://www.alemarati.net/zayed/aldam.htm

(2) Faisal Hamdan "Does the Palestinian armistice still alive". Available at http://www.amin.org/views/uncat/2003/juVjul093.html

(3) Saad Aldein Ibraham "Democracy and Human Right in the ME". Islam & Democracy Study Centre. Available at http://www.islam-democracy.org/ar/4th Annual_Conference-Ibrahim_address.aspx

(4) Al-Quds Center for Political Studies, organized a regional workshop entitled "Reform in the Arab World: Chances and Obstacles for an Izdihar- Scenario" cooperation with Konrad Adenauer Foundation http://vwvw.alqudscenter.org/arabic/pages.php?local_type=122&local_details=1 &idd=49

(5) Ibid .

(6) Mu'taz Salam, 'American Policy and the Arabic response". Al Ahram Center for Political and Strategic Studies. available at http://acpss.ahram.org.eg/ahram/2001/1/1/RE1D14.HTM.

(7) Dr. Abdul Razeq Aldawi, Human Rights between Values &policy. Arabic Center for political Studies. Available at http://www.amanjordan.org/aman_studies/ wmview.php?ArtID=790

(8) Mu"ataz salam "American Policy &Arabic response" Alahram Political Strategic center Available at http://ww.ahram.org.eg/acpss/ahram/2w001/1/1/SBOK48.HTM

(9) Waheed AbdI Majeed . American Policy and the Islamic Movements: Unaccomplished transition. UAE's Center for Strategic studies and research . Available at http://vwvv.ecssr.ac.ae/CDA/ar/FeaturedTopics/DisplayTopic/0,2251,400-0-37,00.html.

(10) Kenneth Katsman ." Democracy is not a magic bullet against terrorism. UAE's center for strategic Studies and Research. Available at http://www.ecssr.ac.ae/CDA/ar/eaturedTopics/DisplayTopic./0,2251,355-97-32,00.html

(11) Hani Nisiarah. "New Librarian in the Arab Region". available at http://www.ikhwan-muslimoon-syria.org/05thakafa_fiker/libral.htm

(12) Al Shura in the Islamic governing system. available at http://www.islamunveiled.org/arb/ree/books/book13/book13.htm

(3) bid (4) bid (5) bid (6) bid

(17) Al- Nabaa net for Information.' Why did Muslims left their task to teach others in America". available at http://www.annabaa.org/nbanews/43/124.htm

(18) Jean liwes Sarbeb. The World Bank and the Arabic Orient after September 11, 2001' Arab orient center for Strategic and Civilization Studies. available at http://www.asharcialarabi.org.uk/center/mutabaat-bank.htm

(19) Fahima Al Saedi . Unity and integration and their effects on Islamic world's economic rebirth, available at http://www.taghnb.org/arabicinashat/maidania/dowal/eqame/13/mq/a-13-04.htm

(20) !bid (21)'bid

(22) Globilization and political Economy, Arabic Institute for strategic studies and research Available at http://vvvw.airss-forum.com/Details.asp?id=451

(23) Dr khalid Shawkat , "The Fetish Collapse". available at http://www.arabtimes.com/AAA/Jan/doc118.html

(24) Ibid

(25) President Mubarak meeting with Universities students and their professors. Al Ahram volume 41902, AUG 27,2001 available at http://www.ahram.org.eg/Arch?ve/2001/8/27/RON2.HTM

(26) Dr. Ahmed Subhi Mansoor."Brothers neighborhood's tree planned in Egypt by Saudis , available at http://www.syriamirror.net/modules/news/artide.php?storyid=9538

(27) Salah Aldien Hafidh. "Freedom is the Critical Situation of the Arabic Media . Al Ahram , Volume 41099 Jun 16,1999. Available at http://www.ahram.org.eg/Archive/1999/6/16/ PI N1.HTM

(28) lbid

(29) Zakaria Niel. 'Did Arab Fail to achieve historical action to qualify them to the new century entrance" Al Ahram Volume 41193 September 18, 1999. available at http://vvww.ahram.org.eg/rchive/1999/9/18/OP I N3. HTM

(30) "America and the Gap between Saying and Action". Via ocean Program. Al Arabia April 22,2005. available at http://www.alarabiya.net/Articles/2005/04/24/12465.htm

(31) salah Aldien Hafidh. Press Freedom between Violence and Terror. Al Ahram , Volume 41715 February 21,2001. available at http://www.ahram.org.eg/Archive/2001/2/21/OPIN6.HTM

Index